Fighter!

The Story of Air Combat 1936–45

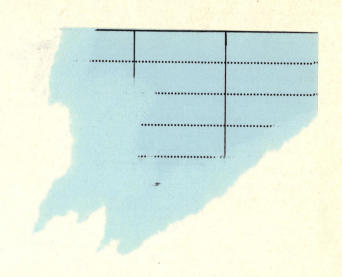

Robert Jackson

Fighter!
The Story of Air Combat
1936–45

ARTHUR BARKER LIMITED   LONDON
A subsidiary of Weidenfeld (Publishers) Limited

Copyright © 1979 by Robert Jackson

Published in Great Britain by
Arthur Barker Ltd
91 Clapham High Street, London SW4 7TA

ISBN 0 213 16717 4

Printed in Great Britain by
Bristol Typesetting Co Ltd.,
Barton Manor, St Philips, Bristol

Contents

1 Combat over Spain

It was February, 1937. For seven months the flames of civil war had raged across Spain, setting brother against brother, father against son. Now, in the snow and freezing mud, lashed by the sleet that swept down on the wind from the northern mountains, men were fighting and dying in one of the bloodiest offensives of all that savage conflict : the battle for Jarama. Madrid was the goal of General Franco's Nationalist forces, and on 6 February forty-one battalions struck hard at the Government forces assembled in the Jarama sector, hoping to smash the defensive shield that curved across the approaches to the Spanish capital.

The offensive failed. Although the Nationalists forged ahead at first, their progress became slower and slower in the face of fierce resistance and the appalling weather conditions until, by 18 February, it was completely at a standstill.

Early that morning, twenty-four biplanes droned high above the carnage of the battlefront. The aircraft were Fiat CR.32 fighters of the Casa Legionaria, the group of Italian 'volunteers' sent to Spain by Mussolini to fight on the side of the Nationalists. All of them, in fact, were serving personnel in the Italian Air Force.

Three of the biplanes, however, were flown by Spaniards – the most famous trio in Franco's air force. Their names were Captain Garcia Morato and Lieutenants Salvador and Bermudez de Castro. Together they formed an elite unit known as the 'Blue Patrol'. On their tails, standing out against the green and

Fighter!

sand-yellow dappled camouflage, was Morato's insignia: three birds, a buzzard, falcon and blackbird inside a blue circle, with the old bullfighting motto 'Vista, Suerte y al Toro'.

It was bitterly cold in the biplane's open cockpit. The chill wind tore at Morato's face as he leaned forward, his eyes probing the dangerous sky above the horizon. Ahead, and lower down, a flight of three-engined Junkers Ju 52 bombers cruised on serenely. Their task was to bomb the enemy's lines of communication; the Fiats were to escort them as far as the front, then escort them on the way back – assuming that the bombers survived. The bombers had suffered severe losses over the past few days, victims of the Russian-built I-15 Chato and I-16 Rata fighters that swarmed on the other side of the front line. They were flown not only by Spanish Government pilots, but by Soviet Air Force personnel too – and by adventurers from half a dozen other countries, including the United States and France. Nevertheless, it was a squadron led by a Spaniard, Captain Andres Garcia La Calle, which had inflicted the most damage on the lumbering Junkers.

Black-and-yellow anti-aircraft bursts blossomed around the Nationalist formation as it crossed the front line. The Italian fighters began to jink wildly, then they turned and flew parallel with the front line, leaving Morato's Blue Patrol to escort the bombers alone. The Italians were obeying orders from their Air Ministry, which strictly forbade the fighter squadrons of the Italian Legion to fly over enemy territory.

The bombers were just beginning their run-in towards the target when Morato saw a cluster of glittering dots over on the left, a couple of thousand feet higher up. They were Government fighters all right; tubby little I-15 biplanes. Morato had time to count thirty-six of them as they plummeted down in loose formation towards the bombers. Thirty-six against three. The Blue Patrol would be lucky if it came out of this scrap in one piece.

Morato waited, timing his next move with a skill born of many air combats. Suddenly, he pushed open the throttle and brought the stick back into his left thigh, bringing the CR.32 round in a steep climbing turn. His two wingmen, anticipating the move, clung grimly to his tail. The manoeuvre took the Government pilots completely by surprise. They broke and scattered in all directions as the three Fiats raced head-on towards them. An I-15 flashed across Morato's nose and he fired a short burst. His bullets found their mark and the enemy fighter dropped away in a tight spiral, trailing smoke.

There was no time to follow the enemy aircraft down to make sure it was finished. The three pilots of the Blue Patrol found themselves enmeshed in a web of darting, twisting fighters, all trying for a shot at the bombers. Desperately, the gunners in the Junkers fought to bring their weapons to bear on the aggressive little fighters that came pouring in from all directions. Already, one of the bombers was pouring smoke from a shot-up engine.

An I-15 rocketed past Morato and he turned in behind it, firing. The enemy pilot threw up his arms and collapsed in the cockpit. An instant later, the I-15 stalled and dropped away in a spin. Sweating, Morato rolled hard to the left as bullets crackled past his own aircraft from an I-15 sitting a few yards behind his tail.

Then, suddenly, the Government fighters put down their noses and dived away, their tubby shapes dwindling rapidly in the distance. Looking round, Morato saw the reason; the sky was full of Nationalist CR.32s.

Later, he learned that the leader of one of the Italian squadrons, Captain Nobili, had defied orders and broken away across the front line to the assistance of the hard-pressed Spaniards. Fortunately, the other Fiat squadron had hesitated only briefly before following suit.

For his part in this air battle, Joaquin Garcia Morato was awarded the highest Spanish military decoration – the Laureate Cross of Saint Ferdinand. But to the young Andalusian there was nothing particularly heroic about his action in tackling overwhelming odds. He was a professional soldier and a veteran pilot

Fighter!

at the age of thirty-three, and he had simply done his duty. Commissioned into the Spanish Army at the age of twenty, he had transferred to the newly-formed Air Arm and after learning to fly on Avro 504 trainers he had joined a bomber squadron at Melilla, his home town, flying de Havilland DH.9s. During the 1920s he had seen action in Morocco, where his DH.9 was shot down twice by ground fire from rebel tribesmen. After that, he had served with a seaplane squadron at Mar Chica and a reconnaissance wing at Getafe. Then in 1930 he had become a fighter instructor at the Military Aviation School, Alcalá de Henares.

When the Spanish Civil War broke out he was in England, enjoying a few weeks' holiday. Returning to Spain via France, he offered his services to Franco and flew French Nieuport 52s until the arrival of the first German Heinkel He 51s. When the Spanish He 51 squadron was disbanded, he transferred to the Italian Legion's Fiat CR.32 group under Commander Fagnani. In December 1936 he formed the all-Spanish Blue Patrol, together with Salvador and Bermudez de Castro. He was to become the top-scoring pilot of either side, with forty enemy aircraft to his credit.

When civil war broke out in Spain in July 1936, the Republican Government enjoyed considerable numerical air superiority. Four fighter squadrons were available to support the Government forces, whereas the Nationalists possessed fewer than ten serviceable fighter aircraft. The total number of aircraft available to the Nationalists was fewer than one hundred; their Republican opponents had twice as many. Republican air power increased still further during August, when the predominantly anti-fascist French Government supplied seventy Dewoitine fighters.

Nevertheless, it was the Nationalists who were the first to receive aid from overseas. On 26 July 1936 Franco sent emissaries to Adolf Hitler, who promised German support for the Nationalist cause, and at the end of the month eighty-five Luftwaffe personnel and six Heinkel He 51 fighters sailed from Hamburg on the ss *Usaramo*, bound for Cadiz. The ship also carried spare parts for a number of Junkers Ju 52 bomber-transports, which had reached Spain by way of Italy. These aircraft were of vital importance to Franco, for they were used to transport thousands of Nationalist troops from North Africa to the Spanish mainland, each grossly overloaded Ju 52 making up to seven trips a day.

Further air reinforcements for the Nationalists came in August, with the arrival of nine Italian SM.81 bombers and the first batch of Fiat CR.32 fighters. The latter began operations from Cordoba under the command of an Italian Air Force officer, Lieutenant Ceccarelli.

Meanwhile the Soviet Government had been making plans to assist the Republicans by supplying arms and military advisers. On 10 September 1936, thirty-three Soviet Air Force technicians arrived at Cartagena and immediately took over various facilities at the nearby airfields of Carmoli and Los Alcazares. Their task was to prepare for the arrival of eighteen crated Polikarpov I-15 fighters, which were then being loaded on the Russian freighter *Bolshevik* at Odessa. The ship reached Cartagena on 13 October, and the I-15s were quickly off-loaded and transported to Los Alcazares for assembly. On the sixteenth, another Soviet freighter rendezvoused on the high seas with a Spanish Republican vessel, which took on board twelve more crated I-15s and then proceeded to Cartagena. That same day, 150 Red Air Force personnel under the command of Colonel Yakob Shmushkievich – who was known by the pseudonym of 'General Douglas' throughout Russia's commitment in Spain – arrived at an airfield south of Alicante. The group included fifty fighter pilots, and it was in their hands that the I-15 – dubbed 'Chato' (Snub-nose) by the Spaniards – made its operational debut on the Madrid front, while the first squadron of Spanish pilots, commanded by Andres Garcia La Calle, converted to the type at Los Alcazares.

The I-15s' first combat over Spain took place on 4 November 1936, when a formation of ten fighters – all flown by Russian pilots – attacked an Ro 37 reconnaissance aircraft of the Italian Legion over the Manzanares river. The Ro 37 escaped with an injured observer, but two Fiat CR.32s which came to its assistance were shot down, as was a Junkers 52. Other Italian fighter pilots, who came racing up to the scene just as the I-15s were heading for home, reported that they had identified the aircraft as American Curtiss biplanes. Because of this mistake, the I-15 continued to be referred to as the 'Curtiss' by many Nationalists for the duration of the Civil War, and it was years before the myth was finally dispelled.

The first big air battle of the war was fought the next day, when nine Fiat CR.32s led by Lieutenant Maccagno of the Italian Air Force attacked fifteen I-15s and French Potez fighters near Madrid. The Nationalist formation included three top fighter pilots, Garcia Morato, Angel Salas and Julio Salvador, and they quickly proved their superior skill. Morato shot down an I-15 and damaged a Potez, forcing it to land; Salas sent an I-15 down in flames and damaged two more; while Salvador attacked an I-15 and two Potez, chasing them off the scene. In all, the Nationalist pilots destroyed eight enemy aircraft for the loss of Maccagno, who was taken prisoner and later exchanged for one of the shot-down Russian pilots.

Strangely enough, the first Russian combat aircraft to see action over Spain was not the well-tried I-15, but a type which had entered service with the Red Air Force only a matter of weeks before the first batch arrived at Cartagena: the Tupolev SB-2, a fast twin-engined bomber with a maximum speed of 250 mph at 16,500 feet. Armed with three 7.62mm ShKAS machine-guns and able to carry up to 1,100 pounds of bombs, the SB-2 'Katiusha' presented the Nationalist pilots with a real headache when it first appeared in Spanish skies during the second week of October 1936; it was not only faster than the Fiat CR.32s that were sent up to intercept it, but it could also outclimb them once it had got rid of its bomb-load. It was a real triumph when, on 28 October, Captain Salas managed to shoot down the first SB-2 – and an added boost for the Nationalists' morale came five days later when Captain Mantelli, an Italian Legion pilot, destroyed a second bomber over Talavera.

The Republican SB-2 units, which were commanded by a

Russian Air Force officer using the pseudonym of 'General Denisov', were used both for bombing and reconnaissance. The Russian bomber bore a strong resemblance to the American Martin 139, and – as was the case with the I-15 – this led to the completely erroneous belief that it was the American aircraft which the Republicans were using. In fact, this belief – which the Republicans deliberately did their best to foster by issuing photographs of the Martin bomber from which the American markings had been carefully erased and replaced by Republican ones – very nearly caused a major international crisis when formations of SB-2s began to bomb Nationalist-held cities, causing civilian casualties.

For weeks, the SB-2s ranged at will over Nationalist territory, virtually unopposed by any fighters. To deal with them, the Nationalist fighter pilots had to evolve a completely new set of tactics. These involved flying standing patrols at 16,500 feet over the front line; as soon as an SB-2 was sighted, the fighter pilots would build up speed in a dive – their only hope of catching the Russian aircraft.

It was Garcia Morato who developed these tactics to a fine art. During December 1936 and January 1937 a pair of SB-2s made repeated bombing attacks on Cordoba, and every attempt to intercept them failed. Then Morato discovered a significant fact; the SB-2s always arrived over the city at the same time and at the same altitude.

One morning late in January, Morato took off to patrol over the city at 16,500 feet, and saw the two bombers appear below him right on schedule. With the sun at his back, he dived on the leading bomber and raked it with his Fiat's twin 12.7mm machine-guns. Pieces broke away from the Russian aircraft and thick black smoke poured back from one engine. Then the SB-2 rolled over and dived vertically earthwards, exploding just before it hit the ground.

Tracers flicked over Morato's own cockpit and he broke away sharply to see the second SB-2 blazing away at him with its nose-guns from a range of two hundred yards or so. Morato dived, then pulled up the nose of his Fiat steeply. The oil-streaked fuselage of the Russian bomber passed a few feet above him and he hung there on the edge of a stall, finger crooked around the trigger and seeing his bullets sew jagged holes along the full length of the SB-2's pale blue belly. The bomber lurched and fell away in a spin, breaking up as it plummeted down and finally hitting the ground in a cloud of blazing wreckage. The myth of the SB-2's invulnerability had been shattered once and for all.

The third Russian aircraft type to enter service in Spain was the I-16, twelve of which – a complete Red Air Force squadron – arrived at the northern Spanish port of Bilbao on 25 October 1936. From there, they were transferred to an airfield near Santander, where they were hastily assembled and hurled into battle on 15 November. Their first task was to provide air cover for a Republican offensive against Nationalist forces advancing on Valdemoro, Sesena and Equivias. The I-16 – nicknamed Mosca (Fly) by the Republicans and Rata (Rat) by the Nationalists – proved markedly superior to the German Heinkel He 51. It was also faster than its most numerous Nationalist opponent, the Fiat CR.32, although the Italian fighter was slightly more manoeuvrable and provided a better gun platform. Apart from that, the Nationalists' tactics were better; the Republicans tended to stick to large, tight, unwieldly formations that were easy to spot and hard to handle. During the early stages of their commitment, both I-15s and I-16s were used extensively for ground attack work, but the responsibility for most missions of this kind was gradually undertaken by the fourth Russian type to enter combat in Spain – the Polikarpov R-Z 'Natasha', the attack version of the R-5 reconnaissance biplane.

Meanwhile, as the Russians continued to step up their aid to the Republicans, increasing numbers of German personnel had been arriving in Spain on the Nationalist side. Their presence was kept a closely-guarded secret. Luftwaffe personnel posted for a tour with the Condor Legion – as the German contingent was known – reported to a secret office in Berlin where they were issued with civilian clothes, Spanish currency and papers. They then left for Döberitz, where they joined a '*Kraft durch Freude*' tour ostensibly bound for Genoa via Hamburg.

The main body of the Condor Legion sailed for Spain during the last days of November 1936. It consisted of three fighter squadrons equipped with He 51s, four bomber-transport squadrons operating Junkers 52/3ms, a reconnaissance squadron equipped with Heinkel 70s, a seaplane squadron operating He 59s and He 60s, six anti-aircraft batteries, four signals companies and one repair section. After settling in, the Legion began a series of bombing raids on Mediterranean ports held by the Republicans, but the Ju 52s encountered severe icing difficulties over the Sierra Nevada and were later transferred to Melilla in Spanish Morocco, from where they made low-level attacks across the straits.

One of the most active elements of the Condor Legion was Jagdgruppe J/88, comprising the three He 51-equipped squadrons. Nevertheless, the Heinkel fighter's limitations soon became apparent; it proved utterly incapable of intercepting the Republican SB-2 bombers even under the most favourable conditions and was usually forced to avoid combat with I-15s and I-16s, although it could hold its own with many of the older types in service on the Republican side. On 18 August 1936, for example, while flying He 51s for a short period, Garcia Morato and Julio Salvador shot down two Nieuport 52 fighters, a Bréguet XIX and a Potez 54 during their first sorties in the German fighter. But in spite of its early success, the He 51 – which already equipped two Nationalist fighter squadrons by the time the three Condor Legion squadrons became operational in November – came off a poor second best as soon as it began to encounter the first Russian I-15s in October 1936. By the spring of 1937 about two hundred I-15s had reached Spain, and the He 51 could no longer carry out its task as a fighter without suffering severe losses. From March onwards, fitted with bomb racks, the Heinkels were confined to close support duties. Throughout the spring of 1937 the Republicans, thanks to the influx of Soviet aircraft, retained air superiority over the vital Madrid battlefront. The Reds had concentrated some two hundred I-15s, I-16s, R-Zs and

15

Fighter!

SB-2s in the Madrid area, and the five fighter squadrons assigned to the Jarama sector inflicted heavy losses on the Nationalist Junkers 52 units operating in the area. The fact that the Italian fighter escort abandoned the bombers as soon as the front line was reached contributed greatly to the Reds' success. It was a different story on the eighteenth, when the Italians belatedly followed Garcia Morato's Blue Patrol into the attack; in spite of their superior numbers the Reds took a severe mauling, losing at least ten I-15s and I-16s for the destruction of three Nationalist aircraft.

In March 1937, shortly after the failure of the Nationalist offensive in the Jarama sector, the Republican Air Arm was substantially reorganized, with many of the I-15 and I-16 squadrons which had hitherto been staffed exclusively by Soviet personnel now being turned over to the Spaniards. The first all-Spanish I-16 unit was Grupo 21, which began to exchange its Bréguet XIXs for Ratas just in time to take part in the final stage of the Republican counter-attack. The other I-16 squadron which figured predominantly in the strafing attacks on the Nationalists was a Red Air Force unit based on Barajas, which was also the base of the Voluntary International Squadron commanded by André Malraux and equipped with I-15s.

During the air battles of 1937, personal scores on both sides began to mount. At the beginning of the year, Garcia Morato led the field with fourteen enemy aircraft destroyed, followed by Salas with four and Salvador with three plus one observation balloon. On the other side of the fence, La Calle had destroyed eleven Nationalist aircraft by February 1937, and Manuel Aguirre Lopez, leader of the first Spanish I-16 Rata group, had shot down ten. Foreign pilots flying with the Republicans, too, distinguished themselves; they included the Frenchman Abel Guides, with ten victories, and the Americans Frank G. Tinker and Albert G. Baumler, with eight each. Another American, Harold Dahl, was reported to have destroyed five, but this was never confirmed.

The performance of the Russian pilots fighting for the Republicans improved markedly with the arrival of the I-16. The Rata

16

Group included notable Soviet airmen such as Ivan Serov, Yeremenko, Lakeyev, Pleshchenko, Boris Smirnov and Stepan Suprun, most of whom were to become fighter leaders during the Second World War. Stepan Suprun, a test pilot, reportedly gained fourteen victories in Spain; he was lost in 1941, while commanding the 401st Fighter Air Regiment in action against the Germans.

By the summer of 1937 there were thirteen Republican fighter squadrons – six of I-16 Ratas, all flown by Russians, and seven of I-15 Chatos, three of which were Spanish – opposing eleven Nationalist, ten of which were equipped with Fiat CR.32s. The eleventh Nationalist fighter squadron – the Condor Legion's 1 Staffel, Jagdgruppe J/88 – had just received the first examples of a deadly little combat aircraft which was to become one of the most famous fighters of all time : the Messerschmitt Bf 109. A second squadron of J/88 re-equipped with Bf 109Bs soon afterwards, the two units being commanded by Lieutenants Lützow and Schlichting. J/88's third squadron did not receive 109s until July 1938; this unit was commanded by a man whose name was to become legendary – Adolf Galland. When Galland was recalled to Germany, his place was taken by Werner Mölders, who ended his tour of duty in Spain as the Condor Legion's top-scoring pilot, with fourteen Republican aircraft destroyed.

In July 1937 bitter fighting raged in the Brunete sector, on the extreme left of the Nationalist Madrid Army Corps, following a massive attack by Government forces. Some of the biggest air battles of the war raged over the front, with large formations of Republican fighters patrolling the battle area and contesting every Nationalist bid to gain air superiority. One of the I-15 Chato squadrons, commanded by Major Yeremenko, began operations as a night-fighter unit during this period, although it also continued to fly daylight missions. Its pilots included four well-known Russians, Ivan Serov, Yakushkin, Antonov and Ribkin, as well as two Austrians, two Americans, a Yugoslav and three Spaniards.

When the Brunete battle began the Fiats of Garcia Morato's

Fighter!

squadron were being overhauled, and it was not until 10 July
that they returned to the fight. Two days later, Morato, Garcia
Pardo and Bermudez de Castro were patrolling the front line
when they were attacked by three Ratas and fifteen Chatos.
During the ensuing battle, Morato's guns jammed and he was
unable to go to the assistance of Bermudez de Castro, who found
himself trapped by half a dozen enemy fighters. De Castro went
down in flames – the first casualty of the Morato Squadron.

On 12 July, the Republicans encountered the Messerschmitt
109 for the first time on the central Madrid front. Despite the
superior overall performance of the German fighter, two were
destroyed by I-16 Ratas the next day in the course of an air battle
that lasted for over an hour. However, two Ratas were also shot
down, together with an I-15 flown by the American Harold Dahl,
who was taken prisoner.

Morato's squadron had a field day on the fourteenth when
Morato, accompanied by Salvador, Aristides and Guerrero, encountered a squadron of R-Z 'Natasha' biplanes escorted by a
number of I-16s. The Nationalist pilots dived through the fighter
escort, which scattered in all directions, and fell on the biplanes.
Five R-Zs went down in flames, two of them destroyed by
Morato. The story was repeated on the eighteenth, the day when
the Nationalists launched their counter-offensive. The Fiat
squadrons destroyed eight Natashas, one of which was shot down
by Morato. On the other side of the coin, a Fiat CR.32 was
destroyed by the American Frank Tinker, his eighth and last
victory, and a Bf 109 flown by Leutnant Harbach of the Condor
Legion was also shot down, the pilot being taken prisoner.

By 25 July the battle for Brunete was virtually over, with the
town firmly in Nationalist hands. During the hours of darkness,
Nationalist Junkers 52 bombers bombed Republican supply areas
and lines of communication, although not without cost to themselves; several were shot down by anti-aircraft fire and by the
newly-formed Republican night-fighter squadron. Two Ju 52s
were shot down on consecutive nights by Lt Ivan Serov (who
was known by the pseudonym of 'Carlos Castejon' in Spain),

and he was promoted to the rank of captain for this exploit. Another Ju 52 was shot down by Serov's colleague, Yakushkin.

The Republicans succeeded in retaining air superiority throughout the Brunete battle, which made the Nationalist victory on the ground even more noteworthy. In the air, the Nationalists had been labouring under the dual handicap of inferior numbers and, for the most part, elderly, worn-out fighters. The six Fiats of the Morato Group, for example, had almost always fought against vastly superior odds; nevertheless, they had managed to destroy nine enemy aircraft for the loss of two of their own number.

The Nationalists learned their lesson quickly. In August 1937 they concentrated most of their air force in the north, in support of their army's offensive against Santander, and achieved overwhelming air supériority for the first time. During two weeks of heavy fighting the Republicans lost almost the whole of their fighter force in this sector, two squadrons of Ratas and two of Chatos. However, when the Republicans launched a new offensive at Belchite, on the Aragon front, there were still plenty of aircraft to support it. Pilots, too, for in August a large contingent of about two hundred men arrived back from Russia, where they had been undergoing flying training. About the same time, another two hundred graduated from the Government's own flying schools in Spain, while a further fifty completed their training in France. In addition, the Republican Air Force included some two hundred Soviet and foreign pilots.

The battle-weary Morato group arrived on the Aragon front on 25 August, straight from the fighting at Santander, and on 2 September achieved a notable victory when they surprised a formation of fifteen Chatos. In a ten-minute dogfight seven of the Republican aircraft were destroyed, two each by Salas and Salvador and one each by Morato, Allende and Careaga. When the battle for Belchite ended a few days later with the surrender of the Nationalist garrison, Morato's personal score had risen to twenty-seven enemy aircraft destroyed; Salvador came second with fourteen, and Salas third with nine.

Soon afterwards Morato was sent on a mission to Italy, and

Fighter!

Captain Salas took command of the group. Despite the Nationalist reverse at Belchite, Franco's forces were victorious on the northern front, where the final Nationalist offensive began in October 1937. Morato's group took part in these operations, led by Salas, and by the end of the month the Republican fighter force had been virtually destroyed. Only four Republican fighters – three Chatos and one Rata – survived the air battles and ground attacks, making their escape across the border into France.

The loss of four Government fighter squadrons in the north was critical, for it meant that – for the first time – the Nationalists had overall air superiority, with fifteen fighter squadrons against twelve. This was demonstrated during the battle of Teruel, which raged from December 1937 until February 1938, when packs of Nationalist fighters roved deep into enemy territory with orders to seek out the Republican formations and engage them in combat. Thanks to these tactics, the Republicans were forced on to the defensive right from the start.

Garcia Morato returned to Spain in the middle of the Teruel fighting to take up a new appointment as Chief of Operations for the 1st Air Brigade. A few days later he received some news which saddened him; his brother-in-law, Carlos Haya, had been killed. Haya was a squadron commander in the 'As de Bastos' group, equipped with Fiats, and on 21 February 1938 he and his pilots had gone to the assistance of some Messerschmitt 109s involved in a fierce fight with about forty Ratas and Chatos. Haya got on the tail of a Chato, but misjudged his firing pass and collided with the enemy fighter. Both aircraft broke up and plunged down; neither pilot escaped.

Haya's widow pleaded for the return of his body, which had fallen behind the enemy lines. She approached Garcia Morato, who wrote the following note to his enemies:

To the leaders of the Republican Air Force, Colonels Don Ignacio Hildago de Cisneros and Don Antonio Camacho Benitez.

On the Teruel front, in the vicinity of Puerto de Escandon,

Captain Haya fell in battle. I am not addressing friends of yesterday nor enemies of today; I am addressing you because you are companions in the same Arm as the deceased. His wife requests his body. I am making her plea my own, and if we should meet in the air one day, before the battle begins I will salute you in recognition of this.

Commander of the Nationalist Air Force, Joaquin Garcia Morato.

Morato decided to deliver the note personally, and on 28 February he set off alone in his Fiat into the Republican zone. Sighting Almuriente aerodrome, he dived low and sped over the grass, dropping his message in the middle of the field. Out of the corner of his eye he saw pilots running towards three camouflaged Ratas, but before they could take off to intercept him he was well on his way home. Morato's note was picked up and its text was published in Republican newspapers, but Haya's body was never handed over.

By the spring of 1938 the Nationalists were on the offensive everywhere and now air superiority was firmly in their grasp. To add to the Republicans' problems, Soviet personnel were being withdrawn in growing numbers, many of them to be swallowed up in Stalin's notorious 'purges'. Thousands of officers, including some of the most promising fighter pilots who had fought in Spain, were murdered during the months that followed. It was an action that robbed the Soviet armed forces of the cream of their leadership – a loss that was to have disastrous consequences in 1941.

Despite the reverses they suffered, however, the Republican pilots continued to fight back hard, and the great Nationalist offensive on the Aragon front in March and April 1938 saw some fierce air battles. The former Morato group was still led by Captain Salas during these operations, and in March the group's score rose dramatically. On the twelfth, eighteen Fiats were escorting Ju 52s when they were attacked by twenty Chatos. In the ensuing dogfight five enemy aircraft were shot down and two more damaged. While the battle was going on, one of the group's pilots, Lieutenant Vazquez, spotted an SB-2 bomber trying to slip across the Nationalist lines and attacked it head-on. It jettisoned its bombs and fled. Two more SB-2s appeared and Vazquez attacked them in turn; one of them began to trail smoke, but before the fighter pilot could finish it off he was attacked by a dozen Chatos. He pushed down the Fiat's nose and headed for friendly territory at full throttle, shaking off his pursuers. Later, he learned that the damaged SB-2 had crashed.

Salas's pilots scored more successes on 24 March, when eighteen Fiats – providing escort for He 51s and SM 79s in a raid on Quinto – encountered eleven Ratas and thirty Chatos. Four Chatos were shot down, one of them by Salas, and the latter attacked a second I-15, which he forced down to low altitude. Every time the Chato tried to turn towards the Republican lines, Salas headed him off with a burst of machine-gun fire. In the end, the Republican pilot held up his hand in a gesture of surrender, and Salas began to shepherd his prize towards a Nationalist airfield.

Jubilantly, Salas watched the Chato begin its approach to land. At that moment, a shadow flashed past him, there was a brief flurry of gunfire and the Republican fighter exploded in blazing wreckage. Startled and furious, Salas had a glimpse of a Condor Legion Messerschmitt 109, climbing away like a rocket. He never discovered which German pilot had robbed him of his captive.

Garcia Morato, finding himself more and more confined to an administrative role, nevertheless took to the air at every available opportunity. On one occasion, on 25 June 1938, he was carrying out a lone reconnaissance over the front line when he saw a group of SB-2 bombers escorted by a mixture of Chatos and Ratas, more than fifty aircraft in all. Without considering the odds he dived single-handed to the attack, building up speed and climbing steeply to attack the bomber formation from underneath. Within seconds two of the bombers were going down in flames; the remainder scattered wildly, their pilots believing that they were being attacked by a large number of enemy fighters. Morato made his escape before the Republican fighter escort had time to react.

Soon afterwards, Morato went to La Cenia to test a new German fighter, the Heinkel He 112, seventeen of which had arrived in Spain. The Heinkels were allocated to the Spanish pilots of Grupo 5-G-5, and on its first operational sortie an He 112 flown by Captain Garcia Pardo shot down an I-16 Rata. Fifteen He 112s survived the Civil War and were based at Melilla during World War Two.

On the Republican side, meanwhile, the Russian-flown fighter squadrons had been progressively handed over to the Spaniards as the Soviet pilots were recalled to their homeland. In June 1938 the famous Grupo 21, flying Ratas, received a new commander in the shape of one of the most able of all Republican pilots, Eduardo Claudin Moncada. His command was short-lived; on 5 July, while leading a patrol south of Teruel, he encountered three Fiats led by Salas. In a brief, savage dogfight two Ratas were shot down, one of them Claudin's. Neither pilot survived.

The battles of the summer of 1938 saw the struggle in the air intensify, with losses on both sides, but the Nationalists never lost their superiority. In July, Garcia Morato at last broke the chains that had bound him to his desk and took command of Group 3-G-3, operating alongside Salas' 2-G-3 in support of operations on the central front. Although Morato increased his score during this period, it was Salas who gained the most spectacular successes; on 1 September, for example, in a battle over the Ebro, he shot down three SB-2 bombers and the commander of the escorting I-16 Rata squadron, Captain Redondo. The latter baled out and Salas circled him on the way down, making sure that no Nationalist pilots took a shot at him as he drifted helplessly beneath his parachute.

The Condor Legion's Messerschmitt 109s were much in evidence during the Ebro battles, operating at their full strength of three squadrons for the first time. Werner Mölders' squadron had now received the latest model, the Bf 109C. On the other side, some Republican fighter squadrons were re-equipping with an improved model of the Rata, the I-16 *bis*. It was as though both Germans and Russians sensed that the Civil War was entering its final months, and that both were anxious to test their newest combat aircraft in readiness for a greater struggle that lay just over the horizon.

By the end of 1938 Garcia Morato's score stood at thirty-six aircraft destroyed. Behind him came Salvador, with twenty-four, then Salas with seventeen. On the Republican side the top scorer was Garcia La Calle, with twenty-one victories, followed by Aguirre with sixteen. No other Republican pilot came near these scores, although several had ten aircraft to their credit.

Inevitably, two years of war had taken their toll. Of the fourteen pilots who had formed the first all-Spanish Rata squadron, No. 3 of Grupo 21, only one was left by the time the Ebro battle ended in November 1938. Of the Nationalist pilots, the heaviest losses had been sustained by the Italian Legion, an inevitable consequence of operating in large, unwieldly formations that left little room for individual action. Losses sustained by the German Condor Legion had been correspondingly small; by mid-1938 the German fighter pilots had developed tactics that were to become standard during the Second World War, with the ‘pair’ of two fighters, the number two covering the leader's tail, as the standard basic combat formation.

In the winter of 1938–9 the Nationalist fighters swarmed over the front everywhere, with devastating effect on the dwindling numbers of Republican aircraft. On 24 December, Morato's group were escorting a number of Ju 52 and SM.79 bombers when they sighted a formation of eleven R-Z Natashas, escorted by Ratas, over Cap de la Serra. The Nationalist pilots dived to the attack, and within minutes they destroyed nine of the Natashas. Three of the enemy aircraft were shot down by Morato. By this time, it was clear that the calibre of the Republican pilots left much to be desired; four days later, the Fiat pilots of the ‘As de Bastos’ Group destroyed fourteen Ratas for the loss of only one of their own number.

In February 1939 the Nationalist fighters launched a series

of concentrated attacks on Republican airfields, aimed at knocking out the enemy fighter force. On the fifth they strafed Figueras, destroying the remains of the 3rd Rata Squadron, and the next day they attacked Vilajuiga, leaving no fewer than thirty-five fighters and two bombers in flames.

The Nationalists were victorious everywhere, and the end of the war was only weeks away. But there was still a price to be paid. On 28 March, returning from his last operational mission, Captain Garcia Pardo – one of the veterans of the Morato group – collided with his wingman, Lieutenant Rogelio Garcia de Juan. Both pilots were killed.

Hostilities ended officially two days later, on 30 March. On 4 April, Garcia Morato flew to Grinon to take part in a film portraying the activities of the Condor Legion. After carrying out a mock dogfight, Morato swept low over the airfield and pulled his Fiat up into a spontaneous aerobatic sequence.

At the top of a climb the Fiat stalled and spun into the ground. Garcia Morato, hero of the Nationalist Air Force and veteran of over five hundred combat missions, was dead.

On 22 May the German aircrews of the Condor Legion bade farewell to Spain in a ceremony at Leon. They had learned their lessons well. Less than four months were to elapse before the roar of their engines resounded in Polish skies.

2 Destiny Can Wait: Poland 1939

It was a beautiful morning. Five thousand feet below the vibrating wings of the nine fighters the silver snake of the River Vistula wound its way through the September colours of the Polish countryside, finally disappearing under the thin curtain of blue haze that shimmered over the horizon.

The fighters, gull-winged PZL P-11Cs of No. 142 Squadron, Polish Air Force, were fighting hard to gain altitude, their noses pointing towards the north-east. From the cockpit of his 'Jeden-astka', as the little aircraft was affectionately known, Lieutenant Stanislaw Skalski scanned the horizon over to the left; the treacherous quarter of the sky from which the formations of the Luftwaffe came to unload their deadly cargoes on Polish targets, their guardian Messerschmitts roving everywhere to challenge Poland's pitifully outclassed fighter defences.

Skalski still found it hard to grasp that his country had been at war for more than twenty-four hours. He was still dazed by the sudden fury of the German attack the day before, in the early hours of 1 September 1939. Both he and his fellow pilots had known that war was inevitable, but now it had come it seemed unreal.

Slightly ahead of Skalski's aircraft and to the right, the Jeden-astka flown by his squadron commander, Major Lesniewski, rose and fell gently on the warm currents of air, its red and white insignia and the distinctive wild-duck marking of 142 Squadron standing out boldly against its drab camouflage. It could have

27

been just another pre-war training flight; any moment now, thought Skalski, they would emerge from the nightmare and return to base for a meal.

It was then that he saw the enemy: a cluster of black dots, sliding low across the Vistula away to port. Opening the throttle, Skalski brought his P-11 alongside Lesniewski's aircraft and waggled his wings, pointing frantically at the enemy formation. The squadron commander waved in acknowledgement and winged over into a dive, followed by the other eight fighters. The wing screamed past Skalski's open cockpit as the Jedenastka gathered speed, plummeting down towards what could now be clearly recognized as slim, twin-engined Dornier 17 bombers; seven of them, holding a tight arrowhead formation.

With eyes only for the leading bomber, Skalski levelled out and sped towards it head-on, crouching low in the cockpit as tracer flickered past from the Dornier's nose-gun. The Pole forced himself to hold his fighter rock-steady as the distance between the two aircraft narrowed with terrifying speed, holding his fire until the bulk of the Dornier filled the sky ahead. A gentle pressure on the trigger, and a stream of bullets from the Jedenastka's twin 7.7mm machine-guns tore into the enemy bomber at point-blank range. At the last moment, Skalski rolled the little fighter over on its back and pulled on the stick, missing the Dornier's pale blue belly by inches. Pulling the P-11 up in a steep climbing turn, he looked back in time to see the Dornier nose-dive into a field and erupt in a tremendous explosion as its bomb-load went off.

There was no time for jubilation. Pushing the throttle wide open, he came up behind a second Dornier, closing right in to fifty yards and firing in short, vicious bursts. Strikes danced and sparkled over the bomber's dark green wings and fuselage. Suddenly a jet of flame burst from the Dornier's starboard engine. Skalski fired again, and this time the bomber's 'glasshouse' cockpit shattered into fragments. The stricken aircraft went into a steep climb, hung poised for an instant, and then spun into the ground.

Climbing, Skalski looked around. The remaining Dorniers had

28

jettisoned their bombs and were heading flat out for the border. There was no sign of the other Polish fighters. Later, when he landed, Skalski learned that the rest of the squadron had jumped a second formation of nine Dorniers, shooting down no fewer than five of them. With Skalski's two, that made seven – and all the Polish fighters had returned safely to base. Nevertheless, their victory did little to boost the Polish pilots' morale. For every German aircraft they destroyed there seemed to be ten more to take its place, and each pilot was grimly aware that if the Dorniers had been escorted by Messerschmitts, the outdated P-11s would have been massacred.

When, shortly after 4 a.m. on 1 September 1939, it was reported that German reconnaissance aircraft were flying over Polish territory, the news came as no surprise to the Polish General Staff. The political unrest of the previous months had given the Poles ample warning of Germany's intention to invade, and plans to resist the invasion had already been in force for several weeks. On 29 August all Polish operational squadrons had been moved from their peace-time bases to specially-prepared secret airfields. But the defensive preparations came too late. Because of high-level bungling and the firm belief of the Polish High Command that a major European war was unlikely to begin before 1941 or 1942, plans for the expansion and modernization of the Polish Air Force had been delayed time and again, with the result that when Poland finally went to war it was without modern aircraft or reserves and with critical shortages of spares, fuel and ammunition. The last pre-war expansion scheme had been approved by the Polish Government in 1936 – to be put into effect in 1941. It envisaged a total of 78 operational squadrons with 642 first-line aircraft and 100% reserves. The force was to consist of fifteen interceptor squadrons, each with ten fighters; ten twin-engined heavy fighter squadrons with ten aircraft each; fourteen light bomber-reconnaissance squadrons, each with ten aircraft; twenty-one bomber squadrons, each with six aircraft; and eighteen army co-operation squadrons, each with seven aircraft. Home-produced combat aircraft were to be the mainstay of the force; new types as good as any in the world. They were to include 300 P-50 Jastrzeb (Hawk) fighters, 300 P-46 Sum (Swordfish) bombers, 180 P-37 Los (Elk) medium bombers, 200 LWS-3 Mewa (Gull) army co-operation aircraft, a number of twin-engined Wilk (Wolf) heavy fighters and dive-bombers, and some 200 training aircraft. Then came the blow; the Government announced cuts in the military budget, and the whole expansion scheme was placed in peril. Air Force Commander General Rayski resigned, and his post was taken over by General Kalkus – who promptly cancelled the order for the 300 Jastrzebs on the grounds that prototypes had proved to be badly underpowered, and ordered more obsolete P-11s to make up for the deficiency.

During 1939, the maximum normal monthly output of the Polish aircraft industry was about 160 machines; with careful planning and shift-work, the figure could have been doubled at any time. Yet right up to the outbreak of war Poland's newest and largest factory – PZL WP-2 at Mielec, which was capable of producing 450 aircraft a year – employed only a skeleton staff engaged in completing a handful of Los bombers transferred from another factory. Incredibly, combat aircraft were still being exported – while the Polish Air Force went on crying out for new machines.

At the end of August, the Polish Air Force possessed some 436 operational aircraft and a personnel strength of 15,000 men. In the spring of 1939, the first-line units had been reorganized around a combat nucleus consisting of a pursuit and a bomber brigade under the direct command of the C.-in-C. of the Polish armed forces, the remainder being split up among the six Polish Army regions. The Pursuit Brigade – whose main task was the defence of Warsaw – was equipped with four squadrons of P-11C fighters and one squadron of even older P-7As; eight more P-11C and two more P-7A squadrons served with the Army Air Force. The Bomber Brigade operated four and a half squadrons of Los bombers – a total of thirty-six aircraft – and five squadrons of Karas light bombers. In the event of a German invasion, plans had been laid to rush British and French squadrons to Poland's aid; apart from helping indirectly by bombing targets in Germany, the RAF was to send one hundred Fairey Battles and a squadron of Hurricanes to Polish bases, and the French planned to send five bomber squadrons.

But the expected help never arrived; the terrifying swiftness of the German blitzkrieg put paid to all hope of that.

By midnight on 31 August, all Polish operational units were in position on their new bases. They were only just in time. At 4.45 in the morning of 1 September, fifteen minutes before the German armies rolled into Poland, three Ju87 Stukas of No. 3 Squadron, Stuka Geschwader 1, swept over the Vistula and bombed the railway line near the bridge at Dirschau, paving the way for the capture of this vital river-crossing by an army task force. An hour later, the objective was bombed a second time by the Dornier 17s of No. 3 Squadron, Kampfgeschwader 3. By six o'clock, flying over thick fog, four bomber groups had been committed to the battle; they were joined by two more in the course of the morning. All told, some nine hundred bombers and a similar number of fighters and reconnaissance aircraft stood ready for the assault on Poland, but because of the adverse weather conditions it was left to a relative handful of units to spearhead the attack. The all-out assault on Warsaw, originally scheduled for 1 September, had to be postponed; dense cloud hung six hundred feet over the Polish capital and visibility was reduced to less than eight hundred yards. And of the Luftwaffe bombers that did manage to get airborne, only a few succeeded in attacking their planned targets. The weather cleared a little in the afternoon, and the main Luftwaffe attacks were directed against Polish troop concentrations which included cavalry. The Stukas and the Henschel 123 ground-attack biplanes tore the Polish formations to shreds. After two hours of concentrated attacks by ninety Luftwaffe aircraft, the Polish cavalry brigade had ceased to exist.

It was in the late afternoon that the onslaught began in earnest, with all twenty bomber groups of Luftflotte 1 engaged in heavy attacks on airfields – mostly the Polish Air Force's peacetime airfields, now devoid of aircraft – ammunition dumps, railway and factory installations, anti-aircraft defences and the Baltic ports. Then, at five o'clock, three groups of Heinkel 111s from Wunsdorf, Delmenhorst and Langenhagen in northern Germany droned over the frontier. Their target: Warsaw.

This time, the Polish Air Force was ready for them. So far, apart from a few scattered combats by small units – such as the action of 142 Squadron – the Poles had not met the Luftwaffe in strength. But now, as the Heinkels and their escort of Messerschmitt 110 fighters approached Warsaw at 5.30, two squadrons of the Pursuit Brigade, Nos. 111 and 112, were already patrolling the capital. In all, there were twenty-two Polish fighters to take on a hundred German aircraft.

Led by Captain Sidorowicz, the eleven Jedenastkas of No. 111 Kosciuszko Squadron plummeted towards the bombers while the fighters of No. 112 under Colonel Pawlikowski took on the fighter escort. The Messerschmitt 110s of I/LG 1, under the command of Captain Schleif, spotted the Poles coming and turned to meet them. Seconds later, the sky was a mass of twisting aircraft and criss-crossed with smoky tracer trails. A 110 dropped away and limped westwards, its starboard engine smoking. A P-11 plunged earthwards, breaking up as it fell; behind it, one of its wings fluttered down slowly, turning over and over like a leaf. Below, the P-11s of 111 Squadron were ripping into the Heinkels. One of the bombers, its cockpit torn apart, rolled violently to port and collided with a second aircraft in a tremendous explosion. Burning debris fell from the spreading cloud of oily smoke. Then, as suddenly as it had begun, the combat was over. Far below, tall fingers of smoke rose from the wreckage of eight aircraft – two Heinkels, a 110 and five P-11s – blazing in the fields. The remaining Heinkels flew serenely on under the protective umbrella of the 110s as though the one-sided fight had never taken place, unloaded their bombs and turned for home.

Ninety minutes later, Nos. 111 and 112 Squadrons were in action again against a second wave of bombers. Two Heinkels went down, one of them under the guns of Captain Sidorowicz, who was himself wounded in the battle. But four more P-11s never returned to base. In just two air fights, the two Polish squadrons had lost fifty per cent of their aircraft. Altogether, the fighters of the Polish Pursuit Brigade claimed fourteen German aircraft destroyed on that fateful September day, but their own losses had been disastrous. Then the fog came down again, providing a respite for Warsaw and the exhausted Polish pilots.

The following morning dawned bright and clear, and began with an attack on a trio of airfields near Deblin by eighty-eight Heinkels of Kampfgeschwader 4. The hangars and runways were destroyed and a number of aircraft – mostly trainers – were left in flames after a series of strafing attacks by Messerschmitt 110s of Zerstörergeschwader 76. The Messerschmitts, however, did not have things all their own way. In a sortie later that day, the pilots of ZG 76, patrolling over Lodz, became involved in a vicious battle with Polish fighters. Two P-11s were shot down, but the Germans lost three 110s.

Then, suddenly, it was the turn of the Polish Bomber Brigade. Towards noon on 2 September, eighteen Karas aircraft of Nos 64 and 65 Squadrons attacked concentrations of German armour on the northern front. They inflicted heavy casualties, but severe light flak and the prowling Messerschmitts sent seven of the Polish bombers crashing in flames, and three of those which returned to base were so badly damaged that they crashed on landing. In one mission, the bombers had suffered over fifty per cent losses. It was a story that was to be repeated over and over again during those early months of the war when outdated, unescorted daylight bombers encountered determined fighter opposition.

The Polish fighters fared a little better the next day, when they destroyed a number of German army co-operation aircraft in the Lodz sector. The day after, however, found the Messerschmitt 109s of ZG 2 providing top cover for the observation machines, and in the course of two air battles the 109s, led by Lieutenant von Roon, destroyed eleven P-11s.

Fighter!

Meanwhile, the Bomber Brigade's four Los squadrons, as yet untouched by the German air attacks, had been bombed-up and fuelled on their airfields in readiness for a retaliatory bombing raid on Königsberg in East Prussia. Throughout the first three days of the war, the aircrews waited in bitter frustration for the order to go. It never came. And it was not until 4 September that Poland's most modern bomber saw combat, attacking German armour advancing on the central front.

The first Los attacks were a complete success. The bombers swept down on the 1st and 4th Panzer Divisions, pushing ahead of the 10th Army near Radomsko, and released their bombs at low level with devastating effect. The two divisions lost twenty-eight per cent of their strength, and were thrown into temporary confusion when a second attack was made by twenty-eight Karas bombers from Nos. 21, 22 and 55 Squadrons. Between 2 and 5 September the Bomber Brigade mounted nine major attacks from airfields between Radom and the River Bug against German armour and supply columns, but no fighter cover was available and the bombers suffered crippling losses.

Meanwhile the dwindling numbers of Polish fighters battled on valiantly. During the first six days of fighting the pursuit squadrons attached to the field armies claimed the destruction of sixty-three German aircraft, many of them army co-operation types. But with the breakdown of the supply system and the critical shortage of fuel, ammunition and replacement aircraft, the air components were gradually withdrawn to the south to reinforce the hard-hit Pursuit Brigade in the Warsaw sector. Only one fighter unit, the Poznan Squadron, remained with the army to the bitter end.

The Pursuit Brigade, fighting in the skies over Warsaw during that first week of September, destroyed forty-two enemy aircraft for the loss of thirty-seven of its own machines. Then, on the seventh, the remnants of the brigade were withdrawn from the Warsaw area to be reorganized. They never returned to the defence of the capital. Crippled by the lack of essential supplies and spares, the brigade ceased to exist as an effective fighting force, and between 7 and 17 September it accounted for only three enemy aircraft, at the same time losing seventeen more fighters.

The turning point of the war came on 8 September. On that day several Polish divisions were surrounded near Radom and shattered by concentrated Stuka attacks – and the 4th Panzer Division had reached the defensive perimeter around Warsaw. In the air the Polish situation was desperate, with more and more aircraft being put out of action by the lack of spare parts and the shortage of fuel. Only the Bomber Brigade was still able to operate in any strength, owing to the fact that its main supply base at Deblin was still functioning. Nevertheless, attrition was high and the last major mission by Polish bombers was flown on 12 September. Scattered attacks were made after that date by aircraft operating in twos and threes, but they were of little significance.

Then on 17 September there came a new development. Nine Soviet fighter-bombers swept down on the Polish airfield near Buczacz, strafing installations and the handful of aircraft that were left. In accordance with the secret agreement between Germany and the Soviet Union – the agreement that involved the partition of Poland between the two powers – Russian troops and armour came flooding into the country from the east.

For the Poles, it was the *coup de grâce* – the final, bitter stab in the back. The following day, what was left of the Air Force was evacuated to Rumania. Among the aircraft that got away were thirty-nine Los and fifteen Karas bombers; ironically, they were pressed into service with the Rumanian Air Force and later fought on the side of Germany during the invasion of Russia. Thirty-eight fighters of the Pursuit Brigade, many of them damaged and only just airworthy, were also evacuated.

During the entire campaign, the Polish fighters claimed the destruction of 126 aircraft. The Bomber Brigade claimed seven more and dropped a total of 350,000 pounds of bombs, but the Polish Air Force had lost eighty-three per cent of its aircraft and thirty per cent of its aircrews.

Fighter!

There was one last act still to be played in the Polish tragedy. On four occasions between 18 and 24 September, Luftwaffe air-craft dropped leaflets over Warsaw, calling on the strongly-fortified Polish garrison to surrender. The Poles did not reply; the 100,000 troops in the besieged city dug themselves in still further and grimly awaited the onslaught.

It was not long in coming. At eight o'clock in the morning of 25 September, wave after wave of bombers and dive-bombers droned over the city, systematically bombing it from end to end. By noon an immense pall of smoke hung over the Polish capital, rising to a height of ten thousand feet and spreading out in a great banner across the countryside. And the assault continued; hour after hour, four hundred bombers drawn from Luftflotten 1 and 2 dropped five hundred tons of high explosive on the city, pounding street after street into smoking rubble.

Early the following morning, stunned by the ferocity of the attacks, the garrison and what remained of the civilian population crawled out of their shelters and stared uncomprehendingly at the devastation around them. They knew that it was futile to resist any longer; that same day, the garrison offered to surrender, and the capitulation was signed on the twenty-seventh.

It was hopeless to fight on. And yet . . . two hours before the victorious German troops marched into Warsaw, a trio of ancient R.13 army co-operation biplanes took off from Mokotow airfield, virtually under the noses of the advancing enemy, and machine-gunned a German convoy that was approaching the city. There was only time for one pass before the Messerschmitts pounced. Seconds later, three funeral pyres blazed by the roadside.

The Luftwaffe was mistress of the sky.

3 Battle in the West: Summer 1940

All that morning the fighter pilots of the French Air Force's Groupe de Chasse I/3 had waited, sweltering in their flying kit beside their Dewoitine D.520s on Meaux airfield, for the enemy onslaught that was sure to come.

It was 3 June 1940; just three weeks since the German Panzer divisions had burst like a thunderclap into France and the Low Countries, outflanking the 'impregnable' defences of the Maginot Line and driving a great wedge between the Allied armies north of the Somme, the armoured spearheads racing for the sea at Abbeville and then swinging up the coast to encircle Calais and Dunkirk. The battle in the north was over now; the remnants of the British Expeditionary Force had sailed away over the wreck-strewn Channel, together with forty thousand Frenchmen who had marched back to Dunkirk with them. But in the south, with the German armies poised on the Somme for the final phase of their Blitzkrieg in the west, there was still a battle to be fought.

The first two days of June had brought fog and drizzle, providing a vital respite for the battered French fighter groups. Now, on the third, eight groups – totalling about 120 aircraft – had been hurriedly reorganized and deployed in a defensive arc on airfields to the north and east of Paris. According to French Intelligence sources, the Luftwaffe was planning a massive air attack on targets in the Paris area, including airfields, with the twofold object of dealing a crippling blow at French civilian morale and destroying as much as possible of the French Air Force's remaining

37

resources. At all costs, the attack had to be broken up before the bombers reached the capital.

The sun climbed higher, and still there was no sign of enemy air activity. The day grew hotter and more oppressive, with a hint of thunder in the air. Then, just after one o'clock, the alarm went up. It seemed that Intelligence had been right, after all. Three big formations of enemy bombers, with a strong fighter escort, had been sighted over Reims, Saint Quentin and Cambrai, all converging on Paris. They were the Heinkel 111s, Dornier 17s and Junkers 88s of Kampfgeschwader 1, 2, 3, 4, 30 and 54 and Lehrgeschwader 1, escorted by the Messerschmitt 109s and 110s of Jagdgeschwader 2, 53, 54 and 77 and Zerstörergeschwader 76 – an armada of five hundred aircraft.

To provide early warning of the incoming bombers, the French had put out a screen of twin-engined Potez 631 night-fighters. The first of these made contact with the enemy over Lassigny, but its crew had no time to make their radio report. The Messerschmitts pounced, and the Potez went down in flames. Two more Potez 631s managed to shadow the enemy formation without being caught and transmitted details of its course, height and speed, but the French communications system was a shambles and most of the transmissions were not picked up. It was not until six minutes past one, with the first wave of enemy already in sight of Paris, that the French fighters received the order to take off.

Among the first to get airborne were nine Morane 406s of Groupe de Chasse 111/7, which took off from Coulommiers just as the bombers were coming into sight. There was no time to manoeuvre into a favourable position for attack. The Moranes raced for the bombers head-on, led by Warrant Officer Littolf. There was time only for one pass, during which they destroyed a Junkers 88 and a Messerschmitt 109, before the packs of fighters were on top of them. The Morane pilots, their aircraft no match for the Bf 109s, found themselves fighting desperately for survival. All they could do was to keep on turning as tightly as possible and wait for a chance to break away.

They were saved by the timely arrival of the Dewoitines of GC 1/3, one of the few units to receive the alert in time. The seventeen D.520s took off from Meaux at 13.10 and climbed hard to intercept a formation of Dorniers over the Paris suburbs. The bombers had already made their attack and were turning for home when the Dewoitines ripped into them. A Do 17 went down, belching smoke, and then suddenly the French formation broke up as the sky filled with Messerschmitts. In a dogfight lasting less than five minutes, Sergeant Robert and Warrant Officer Vinchon were shot down in flames, while Lieutenant Prévost and Corporal Glauder, a Czech, were both wounded and had to make forced landings. Another flight of D.520s, led by Captain Challe, was luckier. Seeing the hard-pressed Moranes of III/7, Challe led his pilots against the 109s and in the ensuing confusion the Moranes managed to slip away.

Disaster overtook the French squadrons everywhere. At Plessis, the Moranes of GC III/1 were taxi-ing out when a wave of Dornier 17s roared over the airfield, dropping a carpet of bombs. Four Moranes were destroyed at once; four more managed to take off, but before they could engage the bombers they were forced to run the gauntlet of a flight of Bf 109s which swooped down to strafe the field. Luckily the 109s disappeared in the haze after one run, and the Moranes were able to land safely on the bomb-cratered surface.

The radial-engined Bloch 152 fighters of GC I/1 and GC II/9, based at Bretigny, fared even worse. Twenty-two fighters took off to intercept a large formation of bombers, but before they could get into position for an attack the Messerschmitts were swarming over them like hornets. Eight Bloch 152s were shot down in as many minutes; the survivors managed to account for two Dornier 17s and two 109s before they were driven off. Another Bloch 152 group, GC II/1 – which had taken off in such haste that the pilots had not even had time to strap themselves into the cockpits – attacked a formation of Heinkel 111s while still climbing flat out, destroying two of the bombers before the escorting Messerschmitts could react. One Bloch was destroyed, but the others successfully fought off the 109s and shot down one of them, followed by a Dornier 17 a few minutes later. Six more Bloch 152s, this time belonging to GC I/8, took off from Claye-Souilly at one-thirty to intercept seven Junkers 88s attacking Etampes airfield from over 20,000 feet. Lieutenant Thollon chased a Ju 88 for several miles, shot it down in a field, then allowed himself the supreme – and strictly forbidden – luxury of landing beside the wreck and picking up a souvenir before taking off again and returning to base. The Ju 88's crew all baled out and were taken prisoner; one of them was Colonel Josef Kammhuber, who was later to become head of the German night-fighter force and, after the war, Inspector of the Federal German Luftwaffe from 1956–62.

By one-forty the last wave of bombers was on its way home. Near Saint-Dizier, forty Dornier 17s and their fighter escort were intercepted by twenty-one Curtiss Hawks of GC I/5, the most experienced of all French fighter groups, and in a violent fifteen-minute battle the Hawks, led by Commandant Murtin, shot down one Dornier, two Bf 109s and two Bf 110s for the loss of one of their own number. A second Hawk pilot, wounded in the legs, made a successful forced landing.

The battle of Paris – code-named Operation Paula by the Luftwaffe – was over. The wreckage of twenty-six German aircraft and seventeen French fighters smouldered on the approaches to the capital; eight French fighters had made emergency landings, and thirteen more had been destroyed on the ground. All the airfields attacked were serviceable again within forty-eight hours. All in all, Operation Paula had not delivered the decisive blow the Luftwaffe had anticipated; but thirty fighters was more than the defenders could afford to lose in a single day's operations, and the real test – when the German armies struck southwards across the Somme – was still to come.

When the Germans launched the first phase of their offensive in the west on 10 May 1940, the fighter pilots on both sides were no strangers to one another. For months, French and British fighters had been in action against the Messerschmitts high above the Maginot Line, as the Luftwaffe sought to probe the allied defences. For these pilots, the term ' Phoney War ' had little meaning. The battles they fought were real and deadly, and they were fought against an enemy already combat-hardened and tactically experienced from his campaigns in Spain and Poland.

The Germans' first blow, at dawn on the tenth, was aimed at seventy-two allied airfields, forty-seven of them in northern France and the remainder in Holland and Belgium. The attack failed to achieve its purpose; in France, only four fighters were destroyed on the ground and the Groupes de Chasse were soon in action.

The Curtiss Hawks of GC I/5, based at Suippes, were in the forefront of the battle. Shortly after first light, the Hawks took off to intercept twenty Dornier 17s which were making for their airfield; the French pilots destroyed seven Dorniers and three Messerschmitt 110s with no loss to themselves. The group had even better fortune on 12 May, when five Hawks fell upon a formation of Junkers 87 Stukas dive-bombing a French motorized column in the Ardennes. The Stukas were unescorted, and what followed was a massacre. In the space of just a few minutes, sixteen dive-bombers were sent flaming into the wooded hillsides. The pilots of GC I/5 shot down twenty-two aircraft on that day alone.

Three other French fighter groups also flew the splendid little American-built fighter, and in the first days of the fighting they enjoyed as much success as GC I/5. Between 14 and 18 May, for example, the Hawks of GC II/4 destroyed over thirty enemy aircraft, even though – because of losses on the ground and in combat – the group had only seven serviceable fighters at any one time. The hectic pace of the air battles is graphically described by the group's war diary :

Wednesday, 15 May 1940. At dawn, while we were establishing ourselves in our new location, we were briefed to fly an air cover mission south-west of Charleroi. Take-off was fixed for 11.00. All available aircraft were to take part; there were only seven. The pilots were selected from the 3rd and 4th Escadrilles: Lieutenant Vincotte, Sous-Lieutenant Baptizet, Sous-Lieutenant Plubeau and Adjudant Tesseraud from the 4th, Capitaine Guieu, Adjudant Paulhan and Sergent-Chef Casenobe from the 3rd.

We climbed without incident until we were over Reims, when we saw a superb V of nine twin-engined bombers heading south-west at 12,000 feet. We decided to attack. They were escorted by half a dozen Messerschmitt 109s 3,000 feet higher up and a little behind. Lieutenant Vincotte attacked, perhaps a little too soon. The Messerschmitts came down on us and we were forced to break away and dive for safety. Only Lieutenant Vincotte stuck to the bombers and made several passes at the left-hand one (a Junkers 88). Meanwhile, Plubeau, Tesseraud and Baptizet were involved in a fierce dog-fight with the 109s; each shot down an enemy fighter and then climbed rapidly to the aid of Vincotte. Together they shot down one bomber; the remainder dropped their bombs haphazardly near Warmeriville and we went after them.

Plubeau's cockpit was shattered by an explosive shell and he was forced to bail out. Vincotte damaged a second Junkers, then he too was hit in his fuel tanks and also had to bail out as his cockpit was filling with fumes and his oxygen equipment was out of action. Meanwhile, Baptizet, Guieu and Casenobe had spotted a Henschel 126 at low altitude, which they attacked and shot down in the forest of Silly-l'Abbaye. In the process Guieu flew through a treetop at full throttle; by some miracle he managed to reach base and land safely with great gashes torn in his wings.

Between 13 and 15 May there were savage air battles in the Sedan sector, where the Germans had thrown a bridgehead across the River Meuse. French and British bombers made gallant attempts to destroy the enemy pontoons and were massacred. The bridgehead was covered by the Messerschmitts of four fighter wings, and on 14 May alone one German squadron – I/53, led by Hauptmann von Janson – claimed thirty-nine victories. Five allied aircraft were shot down by Oberleutnant Hans-Karl Meyer, and three by Leutnant Hans Ohly. Other notable Luftwaffe fighter pilots who scored victories on the fourteenth were Hauptmann Werner Mölders of JG III/53 and Hauptmann Balthasar of the JG 2 'Richthofen' Geschwader, who went on to destroy twenty-one aircraft during the French campaign.

Although the French Curtiss Hawks were usually able to hold their own, often in the face of greatly superior odds, it was a far different story with the slower Morane 406. The story of GC III/7 was tragically typical. On 15 May, nine Moranes of this unit encountered a dozen Bf 109s over Mézières. The 109s, which were a good 60 mph faster than the French fighters, stayed a few thousand feet above their opponents and dived down in pairs to attack, making a single firing pass before zooming up to repeat the process.

Three Moranes went spinning down in flames; only one pilot managed to bail out, severely wounded. A fourth Morane, riddled with bullets, crash-landed at Soissons and was wrecked. A fifth pilot, Sergent Deshons, made a break for it but was trapped by a pair of Messerschmitts; he was hit in the head by shell splinters and passed out. He regained consciousness to find himself still alive and strapped in the cockpit. Somehow, the Morane had made a near-perfect belly landing on its own. The group had just been brought up to strength again when it was involved in another fierce battle on 21 May. Over Compiègne, the Morane pilots sighted fifty Dorniers escorted by as many 109s, the whole massive armada stepped up between 5,000 and 10,000 feet. Although they numbered only seventeen, the French fighters attacked without hesitation. It was hopeless. The Messerschmitts came down like an avalanche and four Moranes were shot down almost at once. Three more were so badly damaged that they could not be repaired. On the credit side, the Frenchmen claimed two 109s.

Despite its shortcomings, some French pilots preferred the Morane 406 to other fighter types and scored a considerable number of victories while flying it. One of them was Sous-Lieutenant Le Nigen of GC III/3. On the morning of 19 May, having shot down a Henschel 126 observation aircraft during an earlier mission, he was patrolling the Cambrai sector with eight other Moranes when they spotted twenty-five Dornier 17s escorted by twelve Messerschmitt 109s. Le Nigen became involved in a five-minute dogfight with three 109s and shot down one of them, skilfully out-turning the other two until they broke off and headed eastwards. The following day he destroyed a Bf 110, one of twenty-five which were escorting a Heinkel 111 formation in an attack on Beauvais. Le Nigen went on to end the campaign as one of France's top four air aces, with twelve enemy aircraft destroyed. Tragically, he died of peritonitis in July 1940, just a few weeks later.

Another first-line French fighter, the Bloch 152, fared even worse than the Morane in combat. Inferior to the Bf 109 on almost every count and slower than the twin-engined Bf 110, the Bloch equipped seven fighter groups in May 1940 and they all suffered heavy losses. In the week of heavy air fighting between 10 and 17 May, it was almost commonplace for a Bloch 152 squadron to take off with eight or nine aircraft and come back with only two or three. By the third week in May the Bloch units had been decimated, and were pulled back to the Paris area to reform.

The best French fighter was without doubt the Dewoitine 520, but this type equipped only one group – CG I/3 – at the start of the battle. Between 11 and 14 May the group was involved in a series of air battles in the Sedan area. By the evening of the twentieth the D.520s had shot down three Henschel 126s, a Heinkel 111 and two Bf 109s for no loss to themselves. The following morning, the French pilots sighted a formation of Messerschmitt 110s and dived on them out of the sun, destroying four in quick succession. All the Dewoitines returned safely to base, despite the determined efforts of a Curtiss Hawk of GC I/5 to shoot one of them down, the Hawk pilot having mistaken it for a 109. For GC I/3, the tragedy was that it was never defeated in air combat; its worst losses were sustained on the ground. Its base was bombed three times in as many days and, by 21 May, half its operational aircraft had been wiped out. Several more groups were equipped with the D.520 during the last days of May, but by that time the battle in the north was virtually over.

All along the front, during those first two weeks of May, it was a story of dwindling allied fighter formations struggling against superior odds, their bases under constant attack. By 14 May, the tiny Netherlands Army Air Force had ceased to exist, while at the end of that day Belgium's entire fighter strength consisted of half a dozen Fiat CR.42 biplanes, operating from an emergency strip near Antwerp. They fought bravely and hopelessly for forty-eight hours before being evacuated to France.

Meanwhile the ten fighter squadrons of the Royal Air Force in France – two of them equipped with elderly Gloster Gladiator biplanes and the rest with Hawker Hurricanes – had been giving an excellent account of themselves. The Gladiators of Nos 607 and 615 Squadrons were among the first to make contact, taking off at dawn on 10 May from their base at Vitry-en-Artois to intercept enemy bombers which were raiding Douai. By eight o'clock that morning, despite their obsolete equipment, the pilots of 607 Squadron had claimed the destruction of seven enemy aircraft. During the next five days, however, the squadron lost ten pilots in action, and was forced to pool its remaining resources with No. 615. The two units fought on until 18 May, when – having just returned to base after a violent dogfight with some Messerschmitts over Arras – the Gladiators were attacked on the ground by nine German bombers, which showered the airfield with delayed-action bombs. Several fighters were knocked out and the remainder could no longer fly because the fuel dump had gone up in smoke. They were burnt where they stood, and pilots and ground crews made their way to Boulogne, sailing for Dover on 21 May.

The brunt of the air fighting over Flanders during the first week of the German offensive was borne by five RAF Hurricane squadrons, whose task was to provide fighter cover for the British

Expeditionary Force. The odds faced by the Hurricane pilots were sometimes fearful – as, for example, on the morning of 12 May, when six pilots of No. 3 Squadron sighted over fifty Junkers 87s, Dornier 17s and Heinkel 111s near Louvain. The Hurricanes attacked out of the sun, and in a running fight lasting several minutes they destroyed five Junkers 87s and a Heinkel 111. To cap an excellent morning's work, they pounced on two luckless Henschel 126 observation aircraft near St Trond, while on their way home, and shot both down in flames.

By 17 May the five Hurricane squadrons had destroyed over sixty enemy aircraft between them, losing twenty-two of their own aircraft in combat and fifteen more on the ground. With no possibility of further reinforcements from England – Air Chief Marshal Sir Hugh Dowding, the C.-in-C. RAF Fighter Command, was holding on to his Hurricane and Spitfire squadrons to meet the air onslaught which was sure to be launched against Britain – the remaining Hurricanes were amalgamated into three units, which battled for three more days until the survivors were ordered back across the Channel.

Further south, behind the Maginot Line, the other three RAF Hurricane squadrons, all attached to the Advanced Air Striking Force, continued to see furious combat under conditions that were growing steadily worse. By 25 May no more than thirty Hurricanes remained serviceable, yet these continued to register successes against the enemy. On 27 May, for example, thirteen Hurricanes of No. 501 Squadron, led by Flying Officer Ted Holden, intercepted twenty-four Heinkel 111s escorted by twenty Messerschmitt 110s and shot down no fewer than eleven of the bombers, as well as damaging three more Heinkels and a 110. During the first week of June the fighter squadrons – or what was left of them – were deployed to defend the ports of Nantes, Brest and St Nazaire, from which large numbers of troops and civilians were being evacuated. Further up the coast, the evacuation of the British Expeditionary Force from Dunkirk was covered by the home-based Spitfires and Hurricanes of No. 11 Group, Fighter Command.

Meanwhile there had been little rest for the depleted French fighter groups. On 5 June the Wehrmacht's Army Group B launched its expected offensive along the lines of the Somme, and on that day the French fighters were heavily involved in attacking enemy columns. Intense light flak took its toll; so did the Messerschmitts, although determined efforts were made by the Dewoitines of G C I/3 and II/7 to keep them at bay. In one hectic dogfight towards the end of the day, they destroyed four Bf 109s and a Henschel 126 for the loss of one of their own number.

On 10 June the fighter groups began withdrawing southwards. Italy had now entered the war against the allies, and when, on 12 June, the news broke that the French Government was suing for an armistice, all fighter units with sufficient range were ordered to make for North Africa. Among the first to leave were the five gallant Curtiss Hawk groups – 146 aircraft in all – followed by about 160 Dewoitine 520s, some of them brand-new aircraft without armament, hastily collected from the factory at Toulouse.

It was left to the pitiful remnants of the Morane 406 and Bloch 152 groups to share the final missions of the Battle of France. Day after day their pilots braved the murderous flak in a hopeless attempt to stem the floodtide of General Heinz Guderian's Panzers, pouring through the Rhone Valley towards Valence.

On 24 June, four Moranes of G C I/6 took off from Marignane to attack units of the 4th Panzer Division. Flying through a holocaust of fire, they strafed a convoy of trucks and tanks. Three of them, miraculously, got away. The fourth, flown by Sous-Lieutenant Raphenne, was hit and blew up in mid-air, killing the pilot.

The armistice came into effect four hours later.

4 The Fateful Fifteenth

It seemed, in that summer of 1940, that the weather was always on the side of the English. It had been so at Dunkirk when, during the last days of May, fog had crept down the English Channel, sheltering the thousands of weary troops of the British Expeditionary Force from the bombs and bullets of the Luftwaffe as they clustered on the beaches, patiently awaiting evacuation.

Now, in mid-August, the weather had once more come to Britain's rescue. The Battle of France had been over for seven weeks, and now Hitler's invasion forces stood poised to hurl themselves across the narrow stretch of grey sea that was England's first line of defence. First, however, the Luftwaffe had to destroy the Royal Air Force, to sweep the sky over the Channel and the coast of southern England. Only then could the invasion armada make landfall and secure its bridgeheads, from which the Panzer divisions would thrust outwards in their familiar pattern.

Dunkirk had been the first round in the battle for air supremacy. High over the bullet-swept beaches, the Luftwaffe's Messerschmitts had first come to serious blows with the Spitfires and Hurricanes of RAF Fighter Command, and neither side had gained the upper hand. In July, following the collapse of France, the Luftwaffe had switched its attacks to British convoys in the Channel, in a bid to probe the state of readiness of Fighter Command, but once again Air Chief Marshal Sir Hugh Dowding had refused to commit his squadrons in strength, just as he had refused to send more fighters to the lost cause in France.

Fighter!

The wisdom of Dowding's policy had been shown when, on 13 August, the Luftwaffe had struck hard against the RAF's key fighter airfields in south-east England. This was Eagle Day, the first of a series of hammer-blows which, it was confidently expected by Reichsmarschall Hermann Göring, commander-in-chief of the Luftwaffe, would shatter Britain's air defences. But all had not gone to plan on Eagle Day; three British airfields had been badly hit, but none of them were fighter bases and the Luftwaffe had lost thirty-four aircraft against the RAF's thirteen. It was clear that a far greater effort would be needed if Göring's objectives were to be attained.

Then the weather, which had been far from favourable to the Germans on the thirteenth, clamped down with a vengeance during the night. All the next day the Luftwaffe squadrons, grouped in a menacing arc along the Channel coast from the Cherbourg Peninsula to Belgium, were grounded under a ceiling of low cloud. Only a few sporadic attacks were made by small numbers of German bombers, but they were enough to keep the British defences on their toes. The weather remained unchanged at dawn on the fifteenth, and the Luftwaffe's meteorologists pessimistically forecast that the low cloud would persist throughout the day. It seemed a good opportunity for Göring to call a conference, and early that morning the commanders of Air Fleets 2 and 3, Field Marshals Kesselring and Sperrle, were summoned to Karinhall, the C.-in-C.'s HQ. With them went their immediate subordinates, including Bruno Loerzer, commanding II Air Corps, and Wolfram von Richthofen, whose Stuka dive-bombers of VIII Air Corps had played such a significant part in the Battle of France.

The meteorologists, as it turned out, were wrong. Shortly after ten o'clock the weather began to clear, and an hour later the clouds had broken up completely.

In the operations room of II Air Corps, just south of Calais, Colonel Paul Deichmann, the senior staff officer on duty, found himself in a dilemma. Bruno Loerzer was absent, but with the Air Corps squadrons standing ready to go and the weather

50

improving all the time, the opportunity was too good to miss. Taking the initiative, Deichmann ordered II Air Corps' two Stuka groups, Captain Keil's II/St. G. 1 and IV (St) LG.1, under Captain von Brauchitsch, to take off for their targets in southern England. Then Deichmann drove at top speed to Cap Blanc Nez, where the advanced HQ of Air Fleet 2 were situated in an underground bunker. The operations officer there, Lieutenant-Colonel Rieckhoff, waved a sheet of paper under Deichmann's nose. It was a signal from Berlin, forbidding any attack to be carried out that day. But it was too late; the Stuka squadrons were already droning towards the English coast.

At Gravesend, the pilots of No. 501 Squadron, veterans of the campaign in France, were on readiness beside their Hurricanes when the alarm went up at 11.29. Within minutes the Hurricanes were climbing hard over the coast between Dover and Dungeness to intercept the first wave of enemy aircraft: forty Stukas, escorted by about as many Messerschmitt 109s. Also heading for the enemy formation were the Spitfires of No. 54 Squadron, which had been 'scrambled' from Hornchurch.

The bombers were met by the two fighter squadrons as they crossed the coast, but the British pilots soon found themselves engaged in savage dog-fights with the 109s and could do little to frustrate the attack. In perfect echelon formation the Stukas swept down on the airfield at Lympne and peeled off one by one, letting fly with their five-hundred-pound bombs. Then they droned away, leaving Lympne so hard hit that it was out of action for two days. The airfield at Hawkinge was attacked, but in this case determined fighter opposition broke up the raid and the damage was slight.

The Junkers and their escorts flew away across the Channel; the Spitfires and Hurricanes returned to their bases, to refuel and rearm in readiness for the next assault. When it came, it was from an unexpected quarter.

So far, the attacks by Air Fleets 2 and 3 had been hurled against south-east England, where the airfields of RAF Fighter Command's No. 11 Group stretched like a defensive shield across the approaches to London. North of the capital, between East Anglia and the River Humber, No. 12 Group stood ready to come to the assistance of the southern squadrons, but so far had not been seriously committed to the battle; while further north still, the area of No.13 Group, extending from Yorkshire into Scotland, was believed to be relatively safe from heavy attack. It was here, under Dowding's policy, that the battle-weary squadrons from the south were sent to rest and re-equip on a rotation basis.

Four hundred miles from the quiet airfields of 13 Group, on the airfields of Stavanger in Norway and Aalborg in Denmark, the squadrons of General Stumpff's Air Fleet 5 had been waiting to play their part in the great air offensive against England. Now, at eleven o'clock on this Thursday morning, they were given their chance. Over Stavanger, the sky was black with aircraft as sixty-three Heinkel 111 bombers of Kampfgeschwader 26 formed up and set course over the North Sea, accompanied by twenty-one Messerschmitt 110s of Zerstörergeschwader 76. ZG 76 was the Luftwaffe's most experienced twin-engined fighter unit. Its crews had seen action in Poland; they had been responsible for the air defence of the big German naval base at Wilhelmshaven during the winter of 1939–40, during which time they had inflicted severe losses on RAF bombers attempting to raid northern Germany in daylight; they had been the first German fighter unit to land in Norway at the start of the German invasion; and, finally, they had fought with distinction during the Battle of France, carrying out escort duties.

Today's mission was the longest ZG 76 had been called upon to fly so far. The bombers' targets were the airfields in north-east England, and – taking into account the distance flown over enemy territory – the Heinkels and their escorts would have to make a round trip of anything up to 1,200 miles. To give the Messerschmitts the necessary range, each aircraft was fitted with a 220-gallon auxiliary fuel tank, mounted under the fuselage.

Although events had already shown that the Messerschmitt 110 was a far from ideal escort fighter, inferior in performance to both the Spitfire and Hurricane, the Germans did not expect serious trouble. According to Luftwaffe Intelligence, most of the fighter squadrons of No. 13 Group had been transferred south, to counter the heavy air attacks in 11 Group's area.

Intelligence, however, was wrong, as the Germans were soon to discover to their cost. Unknown to them, five squadrons of Spitfires and Hurricanes lay in their path. And with only marginal reserves of fuel, the Messerschmitts would be unable to engage in prolonged dog-fighting.

Just before one o'clock, radar stations on the north-east coast of England picked up a large trace, believed to be hostile, about a hundred miles out to sea. The radar plot suggested that the enemy aircraft were heading towards the Firth of Forth, following a south-westerly heading.

In Northumberland, the rooftops of the little village of Acklington trembled to the roar of Rolls-Royce Merlins as the twelve Spitfires of No. 72 Squadron took off from the nearby RAF base, climbing flat out towards the coast in response to the radar's warning. All the while, the fighter controller transmitted the latest details to the Spitfire leader, Flight Lieutenant Ted Graham. Thirty plus bogeys (unidentified aircraft) . . . heading two zero zero degrees . . . altitude five thousand plus feet.

In fact, the radar was plotting a formation of twenty Heinkel 115 seaplanes, which had been sent out by Air Fleet 5 to create a diversion. The main force of bombers and fighters was to have crossed the English coast a good hundred miles further south, within striking distance of its airfield targets in north Yorkshire. The ruse might have worked – had it not been for the German practice of having one master navigator in the leading bomber of the formation. The rest of the bombers simply followed his directions, and in this case the directions were faulty. The Heinkels and their escorts were heading for a point on the Northumberland coast seventy miles north of their intended landfall. No one would ever know what had gone wrong, because in just a few more minutes the navigator and the rest of his crew would be dead.

Ted Graham's Spitfires climbed hard over the Farne Islands, the pilots searching the sky ahead for a first sight of the thirty or so enemy aircraft they were expecting. Instead, they saw a cloud of black dots, growing steadily larger as the two formations closed. Taken aback, it took Graham a few seconds to find his voice. Then he quickly ordered the squadron into a wide, climbing turn, positioning the Spitfires for an attack out of the sun.

The Heinkels were flying at eight thousand feet, with the Messerschmitts two or three thousand feet higher. The Spitfires' attack took the German completely by surprise; they had not expected to encounter British fighters so soon. First to spot the danger was Sergeant Richter, bringing up the rear of the 110 formation. He yelled a warning over the radio and pulled his fighter round to meet the leading Spitfires.

Richter's warning came too late to save 110 leader, Captain Restemeyer. In the fighter's rear cockpit, in place of the usual gunner, sat Captain Hartwig, the head of X Air Corps' monitoring section. His job was to listen to the British fighter frequencies and gather intelligence on squadron movements. Unfortunately, he had not been monitoring the frequency used by 72 Squadron.

A Spitfire flashed through the 110 formation, grey smoke trails from its eight machine-guns converging on Restemeyer's 110. There was a sudden, blinding flash as bullets ripped into the fighter's auxiliary fuel tank, full of highly explosive petrol vapour. The 110 was instantly transformed into a fiery ball, rolling over and over towards the sea. Neither Restemeyer nor Hartwig had stood a chance of getting out.

Sergeant Richter, meanwhile, had found himself in serious trouble. A Spitfire came curving towards him out of the sun, flashes twinkling along the leading edges of its wings. There were a couple of loud bangs, and Richter was dimly aware of his cockpit canopy flying to pieces. Then he blacked out, his weight slumping forward over the stick. The Messerschmitt nosed over and dived steeply towards the sea. In the rear cockpit the wireless operator, Sergeant Geischecker, jettisoned his escape panel and baled out, thinking that the pilot was dead.

Richter woke up to find an icy blast of air screaming through the cockpit and the sea whirling up to meet him. Summoning all his strength, he managed to pull the 110 out of its headlong dive. Bleeding profusely from a scalp wound, he turned and headed for home across the North Sea, keeping just below a layer of broken cloud. Miraculously, he made it. A couple of hours later, utterly exhausted and in considerable pain, he made a forced landing near Esbjerg. Geischecker was never seen again.

Ted Graham's fighters had now been joined by the Hurricanes of No. 79 Squadron, also from Acklington. They swept in from all sides, hammering at the wilting 110 formation.

The commander of ZG 76's No. 2 Flight, Lieutenant Uellenbeck, went into a steep turn to starboard and managed to get on the tail of a Spitfire. He opened fire and the British fighter broke away sharply and went down in a shallow dive, trailing a thin stream of smoke, to disappear in the cloud layer. An instant later Uellenbeck was attacked in turn by another Spitfire. He twisted and turned, desperately trying to shake off the dogged fighter as bullets thudded into his 110. His wingman, Warrant Officer Schumacher, came to the rescue just in time, driving off the Spitfire with a few well-aimed bursts. Things were getting too hot for comfort. Uellenbeck pressed the R/T button, ordering his fighters to drop their auxiliary tanks and form a defensive circle. By this method, each 110 could cover the tail of the one in front. It was their only hope of survival.

Further ahead, No. 3 Flight under Lieutenant Gollob was still keeping close escort with a squadron of Heinkels, despite determined fighter attacks. One of the pilots, Warrant Officer Linke, went after a Spitfire which had just shot one of the bombers down in flames, overhauling the British fighter as it climbed away. He fired a long burst from a range of less than a hundred yards; the Spitfire faltered and dropped away in a tight spiral, but Linke had no chance to see what happened to it because at that moment two more Spitfires dived on him. Bullets ripped into the Messerschmitt's port wing, putting one engine out of action. Linke dropped into the clouds with the two fighters in hot pursuit. Altering course to throw off his attackers, he broke through the cloud base at 2,500 feet and turned for home. A few seconds later he saw, in the distance, two aircraft fall through the cloud layer and plunge burning into the sea. On reaching Jever a couple of hours later, after a nerve-racking single-engined flight low over the water, Linke reported that the aircraft he had seen crashing were Spitfires – but since the RAF suffered no losses in this air battle, they must in reality have been Messerschmitts.

Meanwhile, deprived of most of their fighter escort, the Heinkels were droning southwards along the coast, searching for their targets. As they approached the River Tyne and the sprawling city of Newcastle, they were subjected to a fresh onslaught by British fighters – this time the Hurricanes of No. 605 Squadron, on patrol from Drem in southern Scotland. 'B' Flight, led by Flight Lieutenant Archie McKellar, was the first to make contact with the enemy. McKellar ordered his pilots into line astern and told them to follow him into the sun. Then he led them in a diving attack on the rear aircraft of the leading group. Lining up on a Heinkel, he opened fire from 250 yards. After one three-second burst the bomber fell away in a spiral dive and McKellar was forced to break away sharply as he came under fire from a pair of Heinkels behind him. 'We were by then over Newcastle,' he wrote later in his combat report, 'and I ordered my flight to make individual attacks as I considered harrying tactics were the best way of defeating the object of bombing Tyneside.'

Some of the bombers, in fact, jettisoned their loads over the Tyne shipyards and veered away out to sea. The remainder flew on towards Sunderland, still harried by 605 Squadron. Archie McKellar attacked another Heinkel, which took violent evasive action and got away, then he selected the leading bomber in the formation and swept down in a beam attack, giving the aircraft a long eight-second burst. It started to go down, with both engines pouring smoke. McKellar turned steeply and fired at a Heinkel which flashed across his nose; that, too, began to burn. Looking round, he picked up a straggler and closed in astern, firing off the remainder of his ammunition. He saw the bomber's rear gunner throw up his hands and suddenly disappear beneath his cupola, an instant later the Heinkel's starboard engine began to trail grey smoke. Then, low on fuel and with his ammunition exhausted, McKellar left the bomber to its uncertain fate and headed for the nearest airfield.

During their engagement over the Tyne, the pilots of 605 Squadron destroyed four enemy aircraft and damaged several more. The remainder, under attack now by the Spitfires of No. 41 Squadron from Catterick and the Hurricanes of No. 607 from Usworth, near Sunderland, unloaded their bombs more or less at random and made their escape as quickly as possible. Behind them, scattered along the coast, they left the wrecks of eight Heinkels and six Messerschmitt 110s. It was a high price to pay for failure.

While the battle raged over Northumberland and Durham, the bombers of Air Fleet 5's other attack wing, Kampfgeschwader 30, were roaring in towards Flamborough Head, on the Yorkshire coast. This wave, consisting of fifty Junkers 88s – much faster and more difficult to intercept than the Heinkels of KG 26 – flew in three groups, making skilful use of cloud cover as they approached the coast. Nevertheless, radar picked them up when they were still well out to sea, alerting the defences in good time.

At RAF Leconfield, just inside the boundary of Air Vice Marshal Trafford Leigh-Mallory's No. 12 Group, the pilots of No. 616 Squadron were finishing their lunch when they got the order to scramble. Cups and plates went flying as they dashed for their Spitfires. A few minutes later, at fifteen thousand feet and ten miles out over the sea, they sighted the Ju 88s and swept into the attack. They were followed by the Hurricanes of No. 32 Squadron, whose 'A' Flight had been patrolling a convoy off Hornsea when they were suddenly given a 'vector' that brought them into contact with the Ju 88s. In the running battle that followed, the two fighter squadrons destroyed eight enemy bombers, but the majority got through to bomb the RAF base at Driffield, where they knocked out four hangars and several aircraft. However, there was no escaping the fact that the results achieved by

Fighter!

KG 30 had in no way justified their losses. Air Fleet 5 had taken a bad mauling, and General Stumpff's bombers would never again return in strength to northern England in daylight.

At three o'clock, while the surviving Junkers 88s droned homewards to Aalborg, the RAF fighter squadrons in the south were once more gearing up to meet a fresh onslaught. Radar had detected a large raid assembling over the Belgian coast. It was, in fact, the Dornier 17s of Kampfgeschwader 3, led by Colonel von Chamier-Glisczinski, and this time the Germans were taking no chances. Escorting the sixty or so bombers were the Messerschmitt 109s of four fighter wings, and these were among the best the Luftwaffe could put into the air. There was JG 26 under Major Otto Handrick; JG 51 led by Major Werner Mölders; JG 52 under Major Trubenbach; and JG 54 under Major Mettig. Many of the pilots had begun their combat careers during the Spanish Civil War; they included Major Adolf Galland, leading III Squadron of JG 26.

While the radar's electronic 'eyes' were watching the plot building up steadily over Belgium, another force of attackers roared low over the Channel, flying almost at wavetop height to escape detection by the probing beams. There were twenty-four aircraft in all, a mixed bunch of Messerschmitt 109s and 110s, all of them adapted to carry bombs. They belonged to a unit known as Special Group 210. Commanded by Captain Walter Rubensdörffer and based at Calais-Marck, the group's function was to make high-speed precision attacks on small targets; three days earlier, it had made its debut in the Battle of Britain by bombing three radar stations on the south-east coast, with varying degrees of success.

Now, with the RAF's fighter controllers confused by plots of enemy raids coming in all round the clock, and with eleven Spitfire and Hurricane squadrons already airborne to meet them, Special Group 210's low-level strike took the defences completely by surprise. The Messerschmitts raced across the coast and bombed the airfield of Martlesham Heath, home base of No. 17 (Hurricane) Squadron. One swift bombing run was all that was needed; the Hurricanes returned to Martlesham to find the airfield in ruins, with hangars and buildings in flames and the surface pitted with bomb craters.

Meanwhile, the Dorniers of KG 3 were droning steadily towards the coast, with their squadrons of Messerschmitts weaving overhead and on their flanks. Over Kent, KG 3's rearmost group, under Captain Rathmann, broke away and bombed the airfield at Eastchurch, while the other two groups flew on towards their own target, Rochester. In arrowhead formation the bombers thundered over the airfield, their bombs exploding on the taxiways and hangars and among parked aircraft. A shower of 100-pound fragmentation bombs went down on an aircraft factory on the northern edge of the field, followed by incendiary and delayed-action bombs dropped by the last wave. On their return to base, the crews of KG 3 reported that severe damage had been caused to an aero-engine factory. In fact, they had hit the Short aircraft factory, causing considerable delays in production of the four-engined Stirling bomber.

The attacks of the early afternoon, all of which had been carried out by General Kesselring's Air Fleet 2, had virtually overwhelmed the British fighter defences. The fighter squadrons, scattered piecemeal across the sky, had been unable to come to real grips with the enemy. When Special Group 210 attacked Martlesham, for example, only three of 17 Squadron's pilots had been available for the airfield's defence. The three – Flight Lieutenant Harper, Pilot Officer Pittman and Sergeant Griffiths – had managed to take off with bombs exploding all around them, but only Harper had made contact with the fleeing Messerschmitts, and he had been forced down with wounds in the legs and face. The story was repeated many times over, with two or three Spitfires and Hurricanes taking on ten times their number. Yet such is the strange, unreal nature of air combat that some pilots in the front line flew several sorties that day and saw nothing at all.

In mid-afternoon there was a two-hour lull, during which sweating ground crews patched up minor battle damage and the pilots snatched a hasty sandwich and mug of tea while their fighters were being refuelled and rearmed. Then, shortly before five o'clock, another series of radar plots began building up over the Cherbourg Peninsula.

This time, the threat came from General Sperrle's Air Fleet 3. The attack was led by four groups of Junkers 88s from Lehrgeschwader 1, based at Orleans, followed by two groups of Stukageschwader 1 from Cherbourg. Once again, the fighter escort was formidable; the Messerschmitt 109s of JG 27 led by Lieutenant-Colonel Ibel, JG 53 under Major von Cramon-Taubadel, and the Bf 110s of ZG 2 under Lieutenant-Colonel Vollbracht. At six o'clock, the two-hundred-strong armada launched itself across the Channel towards the Isle of Wight.

Thanks to the two-hour respite, the RAF was ready. Fierce air battles blazed up over the south coast as, one after the other, fourteen squadrons of Spitfires and Hurricanes – about 170 aircraft – engaged the enemy. The Messerschmitt groups now found themselves fighting hard for their own survival and the bombers, left to their fate, suffered heavy losses as they battled their way inland. The Junkers 87 Stuka formations were quickly shattered, and few succeeded in breaking through to their targets. The four Junkers 88 groups of LG 1 were only a little luckier; the rearmost group of seven aircraft, continually harried by Spitfires, was shot to pieces, only two crews returning to base, and only the leading group managed to bomb the sector airfield of Middle Wallop. The other two groups, chased by the Spitfires of No. 609 Squadron and the Hurricanes of No. 32, jettisoned their bombs and headed back for the coast at top speed.

At 7.35 the Hurricanes of No. 32 Squadron were once again airborne from Biggin Hill after a very fast turnround, and were patrolling Dover at 10,000 feet under Squadron Leader Mike Crossley when they were told that an enemy raid was heading towards Croydon, on the outskirts of London. Crossley immediately turned his formation back towards the capital, searching for the enemy.

The enemy, in fact, was Special Group 210 again, whose fifteen bomb-carrying Messerschmitt 110s and eight 109s were at that moment crossing the English coast. High above, their wings glinting in the evening sunshine, weaved their fighter cover, drawn from the Messerschmitt 109s of JG 52.

Special Group 210's target was Kenley, the vital sector station to the south of London. At the same time, a Dornier 17 group was on its way to attack the equally important base of Biggin Hill.

Leading Special Group 210, Captain Walter Rubensdörffer picked out an airfield which he identified as Kenley. At that moment, there was a warning shout over the radio as someone spotted 32 Squadron's Hurricanes, diving hard from astern just too late to break up the Germans' attack. The bombs whistled down, exploding among the hangars and destroying no fewer than forty aircraft. But the aircraft were trainers, and the airfield was not Kenley, but Croydon. As it turned out later, the Dorniers had made a similar mistake; they had bombed West Malling instead of Biggin Hill.

As Rubensdörffer's Messerschmitts climbed away after their attack, Mike Crossley's Hurricanes fell on them. Crossley fired a long burst and a 110 streamed flames, diving into the ground and exploding. Crossley went after a second 110 and raked its port wing, putting an engine out of action. A yellow parachute blossomed out behind the enemy aircraft, and slowly the 110's nose dropped until it was in a near-vertical dive. It crashed in a wood near Sevenoaks, scattering a sheet of blazing fuel.

Crossley's fighters were now joined by the Hurricanes of No. 111 Squadron, which had been on their way back to their base at Croydon when the 110s bombed it. 'Treble One's' leader, Squadron Leader J. M. Thompson, caught the last 110 as it was coming out of its dive, fired, and saw chunks of metal fly off the German's starboard wing and engine. The 110 crash-landed in a field, and the pilot and observer were taken prisoner.

Meanwhile, the other 110s were corkscrewing up in a defensive circle, gaining height and waiting for an opportunity to make a break for it. Suddenly, Special Group 210's Bf 109 group dived slap through the middle of the fray, letting go their bombs and joining the defensive circle. In the resulting confusion, Rubens-dörffer saw his chance and broke away with four more 110s. They were soon lost to sight in the haze.

The Spitfires of No. 66 Squadron had just turned for home after a patrol over Lympne when the Kenley controller came on the air and vectored them on to the fleeing 110s. They caught the Germans just short of the coast and came at them from the beam, out of the falling sun. There was a sword-thrust of tracer, a flicker of flame and Rubensdörffer's 110 turned slowly over on its back. Leaving a thin trail of grey smoke it hit the ground and disintegrated in a cloud of blazing wreckage. Neither Rubensdörffer nor his observer had baled out.

Frantically, Rubensdörffer's wingman broke away – too late. The wreckage of his aircraft was scattered over two fields near Hythe. The other three 110s dived away over the coast, throttles wide open, and disappeared towards France. Back at Calais-Marck, the survivors of Special Group 210 counted the cost of the raid. Thirteen faces were missing: the crews of six Bf 110s and a Bf 109.

So darkness fell on 15 August – one of the most decisive days of the Battle of Britain. Between dawn and dusk, the Luftwaffe had lost seventy-five aircraft in combat against the RAF's thirty-four. It was the biggest blow the Germans would ever take in British skies, and not only in the material sense. For the first time the Luftwaffe, cocksure after a year of almost unchecked victory, had taken a bloody nose. The battle still had a long way to go; but after 15 August, despite Hermann Göring's repeated claims that RAF Fighter Command was finished, the Luftwaffe crews knew that the RAF would fight to the bitter end. And of all the days in that savage summer of 1940, 15 August was the one those who survived would always remember as Black Thursday.

5 Circus over France

The Battle of Britain was over. Operation Sealion, Hitler's projected invasion of England, had been postponed indefinitely. The Luftwaffe's bombers now came at night, striking at Britain's cities in the cold, interminable darkness of the war's second winter.

It was time for Fighter Command to turn from defence to offence. On 20 December 1940, two Spitfires of No. 66 Squadron, flown by Flight Lieutenant G. P. Christie and Pilot Officer C. A. W. Brodie, took off from Biggin Hill and set course across the Channel under a low cloud base. Crossing the enemy coast at Dieppe, they swept down on Le Touquet airfield and shot up several installations. There was no opposition from either flak or fighters and both Spitfires returned safely to base.

During the next few days, Spitfires and Hurricanes from other squadrons, operating in twos and threes, made short dashes into enemy territory. Their pilots reported that the Luftwaffe was absent from the sky. Encouraged, Fighter Command decided to try something bigger. On 9 January 1941, in brilliant sunshine and perfect visibility, five fighter squadrons penetrated thirty miles into France. There was no sign of movement on the snow-covered airfields they flew over; not a single Messerschmitt took to the air to intercept them.

The following day, the RAF decided to stir up a hornet's nest. That morning, six Blenheims of No. 114 Squadron, escorted by six squadrons of Hurricanes and Spitfires, attacked ammunition

Fighter!

and stores dumps in the Forêt de Guines. This time, the Luftwaffe took the bait, but only to a limited extent. There was some skirmishing, in the course of which one Hurricane was shot down. Two battle-damaged Spitfires crash-landed on return to base, one of the pilots being killed. It was an inauspicious end to the RAF's first combined daylight bombing raid and fighter sweep, known as 'Circus No. 1'.

Nevertheless, offensive sweeps were carried out whenever the weather permitted during the early weeks of 1941, and Luftwaffe opposition gradually increased. It was clear that the Germans, following the policy adopted by the RAF before the Battle of Britain, were reluctant to commit their fighter defences in strength. There was also another reason; in January 1941, several first-line Luftwaffe fighter units on the Channel coast had begun to re-equip with an improved model of the Messerschmitt, the 109F-1, but early in February three 190Fs were lost when the complete tail assembly broke away, and the remainder had to be withdrawn for structural modifications.

By March 1941, fighter sweeps over the continent were becoming organized affairs, with the Spitfire and Hurricane squadrons operating in wing strength. A Fighter Command Wing consisted of three squadrons, each of twelve aircraft. There were Spitfire wings at Biggin Hill, Hornchurch and Tangmere, mixed Spitfire and Hurricane wings at Duxford, Middle Wallop and Wittering, and Hurricane wings at Kenley, Northolt and North Weald.

The Biggin Hill Wing, in the spring and summer of 1941, comprised Nos. 72, 92 and 609 Squadrons, all of which had achieved impressive records during the Battle of Britain. It was led by Wing Commander Adolf Gysbert Malan, a redoubtable South African with eighteen confirmed victories to his credit, a DSO and two DFCs. Known to all and sundry as 'Sailor' because of his pre-war service in the Merchant Navy, he was one of the RAF's foremost air combat tacticians, and his famous 'Ten Rules of Air Fighting' were displayed on crew-room walls throughout Fighter Command. Their message was brutally simple.

64

1. Wait until you see the whites of his eyes. Fire short bursts of 1 or 2 seconds and only when your sights are definitely 'ON'.
2. Whilst shooting think of nothing else; brace the whole of your body; have both hands on the stick; concentrate on your ring sight.
3. Always keep a sharp lookout. Keep your fingers out!
4. Height gives *you* the initiative.
5. Always turn and face the attack.
6. Make your decisions promptly. It is better to act quickly even though your tactics are not the best.
7. Never fly straight and level for more than thirty seconds in the combat area.
8. When diving to attack leave a proportion of your formation above to act as top guard.
9. Initiative, aggression, air discipline and TEAMWORK are the words that mean something in air fighting.
10. Go in quickly – punch hard – Get out!

Sailor Malan was not a talkative man. His business was killing the enemy, and the basic skills of his trade were hammered home hard to those who found themselves under his wing. During the Battle of Britain, when he first rose to fame, the popular Press did its best to surround him with an aura of glamour. War reporters found him uncommunicative, and on the few occasions when he did open up his forthright manner often shocked them. Once, he was asked how he went about shooting down a German bomber. 'I try not to, now,' was his reply. 'I think it's a bad thing. If you shoot them down they don't get back, and no one over there knows what's happening. So I reckon the right thing to do is to let them get back. With a dead rear gunner; a dead navigator, and the pilot coughing up his lungs as he lands. If you do that, it has a better effect on their morale. Of course, if you just mean to shoot them down – well, what I generally do is knock out both engines.'

The pilots of Malan's Biggin Hill Wing were proud to belong to what was generally recognized as an elite formation. One of them was Sergeant Jim Rosser of 72 Squadron, who flew his first sweeps in the spring of 1941 and whose experiences were typical of many young pilots.

'We would cross the Channel in sections, line astern, climbing all the time. We always climbed into the sun, which was absolute hell; your eyes felt as though they were burning down into your head and within a few minutes you were saturated in sweat. It might have been just coincidence, but on every sweep I flew we always seemed to head for Lille, which we hated. It was our deepest penetration at that time, and there was flak all the way.

'I will never forget my first operation. Seventy-two Squadron was flying top cover; I was "Yellow Two", in other words the number two aircraft in Yellow Section, and quite honestly I hadn't a clue what was going on. We flew a sort of semi-circle over France, still in sections line astern, and then came out again. I never saw a single enemy aircraft; but we must have been attacked, because when we got home three of our Spits were missing . . .'

No. 72 Squadron's commanding officer was an Australian, Desmond Sheen, who had begun his operational career with the squadron before the war. In April 1940 he had been posted to No. 212 Squadron and during the next few months had flown photo-reconnaissance sorties all over Europe in specially modified Spitfires, returning to 72 Squadron just in time to take part in the Battle of Britain. He was to lead the squadron on sweeps over occupied Europe for eight months, from March to November 1941.

Sheen's opposite number with No. 92 Squadron was Jamie Rankin, a Scot from Portobello, Edinburgh, who had originally joined the Fleet Air Arm but later transferred to the RAF. When he was appointed to command No. 92 in March 1941 it was the top-scoring unit in Fighter Command, and its score increased steadily under Rankin's dynamic leadership. Rankin himself opened his score with No. 92 by destroying a Heinkel He 59 float-plane and damaging a Bf 109 on 11 April. This was followed by another confirmed 109 on the twenty-fourth, and in June – a month of hectic fighting over France – he shot down seven more 109s, together with one probable.

It was Jamie Rankin who provided Jim Rosser with the latter's first Messerschmitt 109. Rosser was now commissioned, with the rank of pilot officer.

'We didn't always fly operationally with our own squadrons. On this occasion Jamie Rankin was leading the wing and I was flying as his number two, which was a considerable privilege. The Luftwaffe was up in strength and there was an almighty free-for-all, during which the wing got split up. I clung to Jamie's tail like grim death, and as we were heading for the Channel he suddenly called up over the R/T and said: "There's a Hun at two o'clock below – have a go!" I looked down ahead and to the right and there, sure enough, was a 109, flying along quite sedately a few thousand feet lower down. I dived after him, levelled out astern and opened fire. He began to smoke almost at once and fell away in a kind of sideslip. A moment later, flames streamed from him.'

A lot of young pilots got their first break that way, while flying with Rankin. And most of them felt the same as Jim Rosser: with Jamie guarding your tail, you didn't have much to worry about except shooting down the Hun in your sights.

Leadership of this kind emerged in more than one way during that spring and summer of 1941. 'Once,' Jim Rosser remembers, 'we were on our way back home after a sweep, heading for Manston as usual to refuel, when the weather clamped down. I knew Manston well by this time, and I just managed to scrape in, together with four or five other pilots. Many of the others, however, were relatively new boys and they were in trouble. Then one of our 72 Squadron flight commanders, Ken Campbell, came up over the radio and told everybody to get into a circle and stay put above the murk. One by one he guided them down, wingtip to wingtip, until they were safely on the ground. When he eventually landed, I don't think he had enough fuel left to taxi in. More than one pilot owed his life to Ken that day.'

By May 1941, fifty-six squadrons of fighters and fighter-bombers were regularly taking part in offensive sweeps over occupied Europe. Of these, twenty-nine still flew Hurricanes, but the earlier Mk. Is had now been almost completely replaced by improved Mk. IIAs and IIBs. Before the end of the year, however, the Hurricanes were to assume the role of fighter-bomber, the actual sweeps being undertaken exclusively by Spitfires. In June, the Spitfire II began to give way to the Mk. V, which was to become the most numerous of all Spitfire variants. The majority were armed with two 20mm cannon and four machine guns, affording a greater chance of success against armour plating. The Mk. V was powered by a Rolls-Royce Merlin 45 engine, developing 1,415 hp at 19,000 feet against the 1,150 hp of the Merlin XII fitted in the Mk. II. Nevertheless, the Spitfire V was essentially a compromise aircraft, rushed into service to meet an urgent Air Staff requirement for a fighter with a performance superior to the latest model of Messerschmitt. The service debut of the Spitfire V came just in time, for in May 1941 the Luftwaffe fighter units on the Channel coast had begun to receive the Messerschmitt 109F, its technical problems now resolved. On 11 May, a group of bomb-carrying 109Fs attacked Lympne and Hawkinge, and one of them was shot down by a Spitfire of No. 91 Squadron.

The Spitfire V, however, failed to provide the overall superiority Fighter Command needed so badly. At high altitude, where many air combats took place, it was found to be inferior to the Bf 109F on most counts, and several squadrons equipped with the Mk. V took a severe mauling during that summer.

Several notable RAF pilots flew their last sorties in a Spitfire V. One of them was the near-legendary Douglas Bader, who flew with artificial legs as a result of a pre-war flying accident. In 1941 Bader commanded the Tangmere Wing, which comprised Nos. 145, 610 and 616 Squadrons, all flying Spitfires, and by the end of July his personal score stood at twenty-two enemy aircraft destroyed. Bader had an aversion to cannon armament, believing that it encouraged pilots to open fire at too great a range, so his personal aircraft was a Spitfire VA with an armament of eight machine-guns. The Germans always knew when the Tangmere Wing was involved in a sweep, for Bader's callsign – 'Dogsbody', taken from his initials – was easily identifiable.

Bader came from Duxford to take command of the Tangmere Wing, and with him, as station commander and fighter controller, came Group Captain Woodhall, considered by many to be the finest controller produced by the RAF during the war. Together, they made a formidable team. 'Johnnie' Johnson, who flew with the Tangmere Wing in 1941 and who later became the official top-scoring pilot in the RAF, wrote of Woodhall:

Over the radio Woodhall's deep resonant voice seemed to fill our earphones with confidence and assurance. When we were far out over France and he spoke into his microphone it was as if the man was in the air with you, not issuing orders but giving encouragement and advice and always watching the precious minutes, and the headwind which would delay our withdrawal, and the low cloud creeping up from the west which might cover Tangmere when we returned, tired and short of petrol. Then he was always on the ground to meet us after the big shows, to compare notes with Bader and the other leaders. Always he had time for a cheerful word with the novices. And whenever a spontaneous party sprang up in the mess, after a stiff fight or someone collecting a gong or for no valid reason whatsoever, Woodhall was always in the centre of the crowd, leading the jousting with his expensive accordion, which he played with surprising skill, his monocle still held firmly in place. We were a very happy family at Tangmere in that spring and summer of 1941.

Handling the large fighter formations which were being pushed across the Channel that summer called for a high degree of skill on the part of men like Woodhall, whose vital role is all too often ignored, or rather eclipsed, in headier stories of air combat. And by July 1941 Circus operations were very large affairs indeed, with as many as eighteen squadrons of fighters covering a small force of bombers. Getting six wings of Spitfires airborne, to the rendezvous at the right time and place, and shepherding them into and out of enemy territory, was something of a nightmare for everyone concerned, and it began on the ground. Three squadrons of Spitfires – thirty-six aircraft – might make an impressive sight as they taxied round the perimeter of an airfield, but with propellers flicking over dangerously close to wingtips it was all too easy to make a mistake. A late starter would add to the problem as its pilot edged around the outside of the queue, trying to catch up with the rest of his squadron.

Making rendezvous with the bombers – usually over Manston in Kent – was another critical factor. A Spitfire's tanks held only eighty-five gallons of petrol, and every minute spent in waiting for the Blenheims to turn up reduced a pilot's chances of getting home safely if he found himself in trouble over France. And over enemy territory the Luftwaffe always seemed to have the advantage. No matter how high the Spitfires climbed, the 109s usually managed to climb higher, ready to dive on the 'tail-end Charlies' of the fighter formations and pick them off. There was no dog-fighting in the original sense of the word; the Messerschmitts fought on the climb and dive, avoiding turning combat with the more manoeuvrable Spitfires wherever possible, and life or death were measured in no more than seconds.

One of the biggest fighter sweeps of 1941 – code-named Circus 62 – was carried out on 7 August, when eighteen squadrons of Spitfires and two of Hurricanes accompanied six Blenheim bombers in an attack on a power station at Lille (always Lille!). The whole force made rendezvous over Manston, with the North Weald Wing, comprising the Hurricanes of No. 71 (American Eagle) Squadron and the Spitfires of Nos. 111 and 222 Squadrons providing close escort for the bombers. Behind and above, as immediate top cover, came the three Spitfire squadrons of the Kenley Wing: Nos. 452 (Australia), 485 (New Zealand), and 602. High above this 'beehive' of nearly eighty fighters and bombers came the target support wings, flying at 27,000 feet. There was the Biggin Hill Wing, with Nos. 72, 92 and 609 Squadrons; the Hornchurch Wing, with Nos. 403 (Canadian),

603 and 611 Squadrons; and Douglas Bader's Tangmere Wing, with Nos. 41 (the latter having replaced No. 145), 610 and 616. The target support force's task was to assure air superiority over and around Lille while the attack was in progress.

On this occasion, however, the Luftwaffe stubbornly refused to be drawn into battle in large numbers. Six weeks earlier, the Germans had invaded the Soviet Union, and many fighter groups had been transferred from the Channel area to the eastern front. Those that remained, seriously outnumbered in the face of Fighter Command's growing strength, had been ordered to conserve their resources. The 109s stayed well above the Spitfire formations, shadowing them. From time to time, small numbers of Messerschmitts broke away and darted down to fire on the odd straggler, always disengaging when the rest of the Spitfires turned on them. Nevertheless, the 109s succeeded in shooting down one of 41 Squadron's commanders.

The bombers, meanwhile, had found Lille obscured by cloud, so had turned back towards the Channel to attack a concentration of barges at Gravelines. A fierce air battle was already in progress over the coast, where two Polish squadrons of the Northolt Wing – Nos. 306 and 308 – had been waiting to cover the Blenheims during the first phase of their withdrawal. No. 308 Squadron was suddenly 'bounced' by about eighteen Messerschmitts, and in the ensuing mêlée two Spitfires were shot down. The Blenheims made their escape unmolested, but the rear support wing, comprising Nos. 19, 257 and 401 Squadrons, was also attacked and lost two Spitfires and a Hurricane. The RAF had therefore lost six aircraft; a result which, set against a claim of three 109s destroyed, could hardly be considered favourable, considering the far smaller numbers of enemy aircraft involved.

Another large operation – Circus 63 – was mounted two days later, on Saturday 9 August. This time, the Blenheims' objective was a supply dump in the Béthune area. Once again, Bader's Tangmere Wing formed part of the target support force, but things went wrong right from the start when No. 41 Squadron failed to rendezvous on time. The remainder, unable to wait,

71

carried on across the Channel. For a while, all was peaceful; then, just a few miles short of the target, the 109s hit them hard. For the next few minutes, Bader's pilots were hard put to it to hold their own, the wing becoming badly dislocated as the Messerschmitts pressed home a series of determined attacks. Bader misjudged an attack on a 109 and suddenly found himself isolated. Six enemy fighters closed in on him and, by superb flying, he destroyed two. The end came soon afterwards, when a third 109 collided with him and severed his Spitfire's fuselage just behind the cockpit. Bader managed to struggle clear of the plunging debris, leaving one of his artificial legs still trapped in the cockpit. His parachute opened, and he floated down to a painful landing and captivity.

On 12 August, three days after Bader was shot down, the medium bombers of the RAF's No. 2 Group made their deepest daylight penetration into enemy territory so far when 54 Blenheims bombed two power stations near Cologne. They were escorted by Westland Whirlwind fighters of No. 263 Squadron, the only fighter aircraft with sufficient range to carry out this task. The Whirlwind was highly manoeuvrable, faster than a Spitfire at low altitude, and its armament of four closely-grouped 20mm nose cannon made it a match for any Luftwaffe fighter of the day. As it was, the Whirlwind experienced a spate of troubles with its twin Rolls-Royce Peregrine engines, and only two squadrons were equipped with the type. Eventually, it was used in the fighter-bomber role with considerable success.

As August gave way to September, some senior Air Staff members began to have serious doubts about the value of Circus operations. Fighter Command losses were climbing steadily, and the results achieved hardly seemed to compensate for them. The only real justification for continuing the sweeps, apparently, was to ensure that Fighter Command remained in a state of combat readiness.

The morale of Fighter Command, however, was soon to take a serious blow. On 21 September 1941, Polish pilots of No. 315 Squadron, on their way home after Circus 101, reported being attacked by 'an unknown enemy aircraft with a radial engine'. A few days later, Jim Rosser of 72 Squadron was on a sweep over Boulogne, flying No. 2 to Ken Campbell, when he too sighted one of the mysterious radial-engined machines and went down after it, opening fire at extreme range. The enemy aircraft dived into the Boulogne flak barrage and Campbell called Rosser back, but not before the latter had secured some good gun-camera shots.

All sorts of wild rumours circulated in Fighter Command, the favourite among them being that the strange aircraft were Curtiss Hawks, captured by the Germans and pressed into service. Then RAF Intelligence examined all the data and came up with the answer. The Focke-Wulf 190 had arrived in France.

The first Luftwaffe unit to receive Focke-Wulf 190s on the Channel coast was Jagdgeschwader 26, followed by JG 2, and by October 1941 the RAF was encountering the type in growing numbers. Within weeks, the FW 190 had established a definite measure of air superiority for the Germans. It completely out-classed the Spitfire VB at all altitudes, and Fighter Command losses rose steadily that autumn. Not until the advent of the Spitfire IX – resulting from the marriage of a Merlin 61 engine to a Mk. V airframe – was the balance restored; but the first Mk. IXs did not enter service with No. 64 Squadron until June 1942.

As far as Circus operations were concerned, the crunch came on 8 November 1941, when the Blenheims of No. 2 Group and their escorting fighters suffered unusually heavy losses. The whole 'show' went wrong from the start, with poor visibility making it difficult for the bombers and fighters to rendezvous as planned. Combined with a general lack of co-ordination, this meant that the attacking forces entered enemy territory piecemeal, and the Focke-Wulfs and Messerschmitts were waiting for them. The Intelligence Summary of No. 118 (Spitfire) Squadron gives a typical account:

It was decided in the afternoon to carry out a most ill-conceived scheme, designated Rodeo 5, in which the Middle Wallop

Fighter!

> Wing rendezvoused with the Whirlwinds of 263 Squadron over Warmwell and carried out a sweep of the Channel Islands area. The whole sortie seems to have been one long muddle. The Whirlwinds led the Spits much too far south and then returned right over the flak area. 501 Squadron were sent out to deal with a few Huns that put in an appearance when we were on the way back. 118 went back to help, but 501 were not located. The net result was at least three planes damaged by flak and enemy aircraft, and one shot down, and all we could claim was one enemy aircraft damaged . . .

It was the end. Winston Churchill himself decreed that there should be no more large-scale sweeps over the Continent in 1941; it was now the duty of Fighter Command to gather its strength for the following spring.

By that time, although no one yet dreamed it, Britain would no longer stand alone. On the other side of the world, events were moving to a climax that would soon make Pearl Harbor a household name, and bring the unparalleled resources of the United States into the battle.

6 Flying Tigers:
The American Volunteer
Group 1941–2

23 December 1941 was a day that would live in many memories. On that day, for the first time since 1918, British and American airmen stood shoulder to shoulder against a common enemy.

It was two weeks now since Vice-Admiral Nagumo's six fleet carriers had launched their devastating air strikes against Pearl Harbor, leaving the battle squadron of the United States Pacific Fleet in ruins. Everywhere the Japanese were on the offensive. On the same day that Pearl Harbor was attacked, their forces landed in Thailand and on the north-east coast of Malaya; the next day, they began their assault on Hong Kong; and on 10 December, their bombers inflicted yet another shattering naval defeat on the Allies when they sank two of the British Navy's finest battleships, HMS *Prince of Wales* and HMS *Repulse*.

With Thailand secured, it was only a question of time before the Japanese opened an offensive in Burma, carving out a road towards the real prize in south-east Asia: India. And when the air-raid sirens wailed for the first time in Burma's capital, Rangoon, on 23 December, there was little doubt that they heralded a series of major air attacks designed to 'soften up' the country's already overstretched defences.

As far as the Japanese knew, responsibility for the defence of the Rangoon area rested on a single RAF fighter squadron: No. 67, equipped with American-built Brewster Buffaloes. The tubby little Buffalo had been used with considerable success by Finnish pilots against the Russians during the Winter War of 1939–40,

75

but it was no match against the Mitsubishi Zero fighter, as the RAF and RAAF squadrons using it in Malaya had already found to their cost. So, when the Japanese sent thirty bombers to attack Rangoon on this morning of 23 December, they were certain that their escort of twenty fighters – not Zeros this time, but earlier Nakajima Ki.27s – would be more than enough to handle the dozen or so RAF fighters they expected to encounter.

The Japanese were unaware that the sixteen-strong RAF fighter squadron on Mingaladon airfield, near Rangoon, had recently been joined by twenty-one much more modern aircraft. They were Curtiss P-40B Tomahawks; single-seat fighters armed with six .30-inch Colt-Browning machine-guns and powered by Allison V-1710 in-line engines giving them a maximum speed of 350 mph. On their wings they bore the insignia of the Chinese Air Force, a twelve-pointed white star on a blue disc, but the men who flew them were Americans. The P-40s, in fact, belonged to the 3rd Pursuit Squadron of the American Volunteer Group, a remarkable fighting unit whose courage, skill and aggressive spirit were to be a shining example to Allied airmen everywhere during those dark early days of the war in the east.

The origins of the American Volunteer Group went back to May 1937, when a retired United States Army Air Corps officer named Claire Chennault arrived in China at the request of Chiang Kai-shek's government to carry out a survey of the Chinese Air Force. Chennault, whose controversial views on air defence had not endeared him to many colleagues in the USA, expected to remain in China for only a few months. He had no inkling that China would be his home for eight years, until the final defeat of Japan in 1945.

Chennault was appalled by what he saw as he toured the Chinese Air Force's training schools during that summer of 1937. The quality of both pilots and equipment was terrible. At Loyang, one of the principal flying schools, where the instructors were Italian, cadets graduated whether they could fly adequately or not.

The shortcomings became brutally apparent in July 1937,

when Japanese forces invaded Manchuria and began pushing inland along the Yangtse river. Although the Chinese Air Force had 500 aircraft, only 91 were airworthy and only a handful of pilots were fit to fly them in action. The first skirmishes with the highly-trained Japanese showed not only that the Chinese Air Force had no means of slowing down the enemy advance, but that it was also totally incapable of defending China's cities against air attack. Within weeks, the Japanese had gained complete air superiority, and for the next three years they were to use north-east China as a virtual operational training area for their combat pilots. It was small wonder that the Japanese Army and Navy Air Forces, by December 1941, were tactically among the world's best.

By October 1937, following bitter fighting in the Shanghai sector, the effective strength of the Chinese Air Force was twelve aircraft. In a desperate bid to save the situation an international air squadron was formed, composed of British, Dutch and American volunteers and armed with a motley collection of aircraft purchased by an American arms dealer. Although the squadron flew many missions during the winter of 1937–8, it was hopelessly outclassed and its operations came to an abrupt end early in 1938, when its base at Hankow was destroyed.

It was the Russians who brought the first real aid to the Chinese. Late in 1937, six Soviet Air Force squadrons – four of fighters and two of bombers – were sent to China, together with 350 'advisers'. The commander of the Russian contingent was Suprun, fresh from his tour of duty in Spain. Operating a mixture of I-15 and I-16 fighters, the Russians went into action early in 1938, fighting hard and continuously until early March, when they were withdrawn for a rest. Their place was taken by the first batch of Russian-trained Chinese pilots, who were flung into action in the defence of Nanking, but once again they proved no match for the Japanese and they were decimated.

Between 1937 and 1940, it was the Russians who provided the nucleus of China's air defences. Soviet air strength in China increased all the time, and when Japanese troops invaded

Mongolian territory in the summer of 1939 they met the attack with 580 aircraft, including 350 fighters. The Japanese, on the other hand, had some 450 combat aircraft in Manchuria, and when the two sides clashed some of the biggest air battles the world had seen since 1918 took place over the Khalkhin river.

By this time, several Russian squadrons had exchanged their I-15s for the more modern I-153, with a retractable undercarriage, and the appearance of these aircraft over the Khalkhin took the Japanese fighter pilots completely by surprise. The Russians would approach the combat area with their undercarriages lowered, giving the impression that they were slower I-15s and inviting the Japanese to attack them. Once the enemy had committed themselves, the Russians would pull up their landing gear and neatly turn the tables.

Occasionally, the sky over the river was covered by a twisting mêlée of up to two hundred aircraft as big formations clashed head-on. The Japanese usually emerged the worse from these encounters; although their principal fighter type, the Nakajima Ki.27, could hold its own against the I-153, it was outclassed in speed and firepower by its most frequent opponent – the I-16, which the Japanese dubbed 'Abu' (Gadfly). Although there was not a great deal of difference in terms of skill between Russian and Japanese pilots, Russian tactics were generally better – the result of lessons learned in Spain. The armament of their fighters was better, too; 7.62mm machine-guns carried by the I-16 compared with the twin 7.7mm weapons mounted in both the Ki.27 and the Mitsubishi A5M. The I-153 also had four 7.62s, as well as provision for six RS-82 air-to-ground rockets under the wings. On more than one occasion over the Khalkhin, RS-82s were launched at Japanese fighters in the course of a dogfight.

The fighting between the Russians and Japanese petered out in the autumn of 1939. Japan had planned further offensives into Mongolia, but was persuaded to call off the idea by her ally, Germany, who – with the attack on Poland in the offing – was anxious to maintain friendly relations with the Soviet Union. This left the Japanese free to step up their air attacks on targets in south-west China, and by the summer of 1940 the situation was once more critical.

Claire Chennault had now been in the country for three years, acting as an air adviser to Chiang Kai-shek and making a careful study of the tactics emerging from the fighting in the north. He now held the rank of colonel in the Chinese Air Force and worked in close conjunction with Mao Pang-tso, the CAF's Director of Operations. In October 1940, both men were summoned to a conference with Chiang Kai-shek, who proposed sending them on a mission to the United States to buy American fighters and hire the pilots to fly them.

Chennault's 'shopping list' envisaged the purchase of 660 aircraft, 500 of them combat types, enough materials to build 14 large airfields and 122 landing strips, plus ammunition and spares for a year's operational flying. Officials of the US Presidential Liaison Committee, which had to approve the purchase of arms for overseas countries in the United States, viewed the proposals with incredulity when Chennault and Mao presented them in November 1940. America's aviation industry was already working flat out to provide modern combat aircraft for the nation's own army and navy, as well as for Great Britain, and the Pentagon's military leaders were initially opposed to the idea of providing badly-needed hardware for a remote conflict.

They had reckoned, however, without the determination of Claire Chennault. He spent the next few weeks drumming up support in the White House. He acquired a group of powerful backers, including Henry Morgenthau, Secretary of the Treasury, and in the end persuaded President Roosevelt himself to give his blessing to the scheme. With White House approval secured, Chennault and Mao began an extensive tour of aircraft factories throughout the United States, in search of suitable combat aircraft. It was a far from easy task. The demands of the US armed forces outstripped production, and the Royal Air Force had first priority among overseas customers. For a time, it looked as though Chennault would return to China empty-handed. Then Burdette Wright, vice-president of the Curtiss-Wright Aircraft

Corporation, and William D. Pawley – the arms agent who had supplied aircraft for the International Air Squadron – came to his rescue. Between them, they arranged for Chennault to purchase one hundred P-40B fighters. These had originally been offered to the RAF, but had been rejected on the grounds that they were not sufficiently advanced. The RAF finally settled for the improved P-40E version, and in January 1941 the P-40Bs were sold to the Chinese Government at a cost of nearly nine million dollars.

While the fighters were being crated for delivery, Chennault set about recruiting volunteers. The whole operation went ahead in strict secrecy, recruitment being carried out under cover by the Central Aircraft Manufacturing Company (CAMCO). Between April and July 1941, CAMCO agents toured American air bases in search of volunteers for the AVG. They offered pilots a salary of between $600 and $750 per month, plus expenses, accommodation and thirty days' paid annual leave. Also – although this never appeared in the contract, for obvious reasons – pilots were promised a bonus of $500 for every Japanese aircraft they destroyed. Ground crews were offered salaries ranging between $150 and $350 per month, depending on their skills.

The volunteers, all of them serving US military personnel, were bound to CAMCO by a one-year contract. They would retain their American citizenship, and after their service in China they would return to their military units with no loss of seniority.

By the end of June 1941 CAMCO's agents had recruited 100 pilots and 150 mechanics. Not all of them were as experienced as Chennault would have wished, but finding volunteers had proved more difficult than he had expected and some compromise had been necessary.

The first contingent of volunteers arrived in Rangoon on 28 July and from there went to Kyedaw airfield, 170 miles further north. Chennault had originally planned to use Kunming in China as the AVG's main operational base, but this field was not completed in time and so Kyedaw had to be used as an alternative, with the tacit approval of the British War Office and the colonial administration in Burma. Conditions at Kyedaw were frightful, with tropical diseases such as malaria and dysentery rife in the hot, humid climate, and illness was a perpetual battle with which the Americans – some of whom had never been overseas before – had to contend.

The training programme was hard, too. For a start, not many of the volunteers were experienced fighter pilots, so they all had to start virtually from scratch. Then, to their astonishment, Chennault told them to forget the air fighting tactics they had been taught in the United States. Combat flying would be based on the 'pair', with the lead aircraft attacking and the number two guarding his tail – tactics pioneered by the German aces of the First World War, and still used successfully by their successors in the European air war. Day after day the AVG pilots flew and trained until Chennault's air fighting rules were second nature to them. Then, and only then, did they begin to study the enemy's tactics.

It was now that Chennault's careful study of Japanese airmen in action paid dividends. First of all, he hammered home the lesson that, far from being second-rate as portrayed in western circles, the Japanese were excellent, highly-trained pilots whose air combat discipline was second to none. Their handling of large bomber formations was particularly good, so Chennault trained his men to break up such formations and destroy their cohesion. Marksmanship was of vital importance, and AVG pilots spent hours poring over drawings of the enemy bombers they were likely to encounter, picking out vulnerable spots such as the fuel tanks, which in most Japanese types were inadequately protected.

As far as combat with enemy fighters was concerned, Chennault stressed that the Nakajima and Mitsubishi types were more manoeuvrable than the P-40, so he taught his pilots to make use of the American fighter's heavier weight and higher speed by making fast diving attacks. A short, accurately-placed burst from the P-40's six machine-guns would usually be sufficient to cripple a less robust opponent.

Fighter!

Volunteer Group pilots spent some seventy-two hours working on these tactics in the classroom, followed by at least sixty hours of air fighting practice. They learned to cruise in pairs at maximum altitude and make high-speed passes at simulated enemy aircraft below, avoiding turning manoeuvres and fighting on the climb-and-dive. Inevitably, with spare parts in short supply, this arduous training took its toll of the P-40s; by the first week of December 1941, only fifty-five of the original 100 aircraft were serviceable.

Gradually, a formidable esprit de corps grew among the A V G personnel as their confidence increased. By December, Chennault had forged them into a highly efficient fighting unit, yet the pretence of being civilian employees under contract was still carefully fostered. There were no ranks as such. Pilots were designated by the position they held within the organization, such as squadron leader, flight leader and wingman.

Soon after the Japanese attack on Pearl Harbor, it was decided to divide the resources of the A V G. Kyedaw airfield was abandoned, and on 10 December twenty-one P-40s flew to Mingaladon, near Rangoon, under the command of Squadron Leader Arivs Olson. The other thirty-four airworthy machines, led by Squadron Leader Robert Sandell, flew north-east to the now completed base at Kunming, close to China's lifeline: the vital Burma Road.

It was Robert Sandell's 1st Pursuit Squadron which first made contact with the enemy. It happened on the morning of 20 December, when ten P-40s were 'scrambled' to intercept a force of Japanese bombers heading for Kunming. The enemy had apparently not expected fighter opposition, for the ten twin-engined Mitsubishi Ki. 21 bombers were unescorted. Sandell's pilots had a field day; six bombers went down in flames as the P-40s ripped into their formation. Only one P-40 failed to return; its pilot, Ed Rector, made a successful forced landing.

At Mingaladon, the men of Arivs Olson's 3rd Pursuit Squadron heard of this victory with envy and wondered when their turn would come. They did not have long to wait. On the twenty-third, the Japanese appeared over Rangoon in strength and the AVG took off to intercept them, accompanied by the RAF's Buffaloes. While the latter took on the escorting Ki.27 fighters, Olsen's twelve P-40s dived on the bomber formation. The first AVG pilot to score was Ken Jernstedt, who chopped away at a Mitsubishi until it went down with both engines streaming flames. His colleague, Charles Older, fired at a second bomber and found himself flying through a cloud of smoke and debris as the enemy's bomb-load exploded, scattering wreckage across the sky. Fierce battles raged over Rangoon as the American and British pilots pressed home their attacks. They destroyed six bombers and four fighters, but the RAF lost five Buffaloes and the AVG four P-40s. Two American pilots baled out and were saved, although one of them – Flight Leader Paul J. Greene – had some nasty moments when a Japanese fighter took a shot at him as he floated down under his parachute. Fortunately, the enemy pilot's aim was poor.

The Americans avenged their losses on Christmas Day, when the Japanese mounted a second major raid on Rangoon with sixty bombers escorted by twenty fighters. The enemy formation split up some distance away from the city, one half heading for Mingaladon airfield and the other for Rangoon's docks. This time, the Allied pilots had received plenty of warning of the attack, and while the RAF's Buffaloes provided top cover over Rangoon the AVG's thirteen P-40s made contact with the enemy ten miles away. The Americans had the advantage of height, and while one P-40 flight attacked the fighter escort – composed of Zeros on this occasion – the rest tore into the bombers, using Chennault's tactics to good effect.

Within minutes, the impeccable Japanese formation had been torn to shreds, and the AVG's first three fighter aces had been created. Charles Older destroyed four bombers; Robert P. ('Duke') Hedman got four bombers and a Zero; and three bombers fell to the guns of Robert T. Smith. Not a bad day's work for a retired acrobat, as Smith had fictitiously registered himself en route to Burma from the United States!

Fighter!

As the Japanese bombers scattered the A V G pilots fell upon them, shooting one after another out of the sky. Eighteen bombers and six fighters fell burning into the Burmese countryside; over Rangoon, the jubilant pilots of No. 67 Squadron R A F accounted for twelve more.

Two P-40s were lost, but both pilots escaped. One of them, William E. Bartling, made a forced landing beside a railway line. Five minutes later, he was drinking a well-earned glass of beer in a railway coach, the mobile home of an English railroad overseer. The second pilot, Parker S. Dupouy, had a more traumatic experience. He shot down two bombers, then collided with a Zero in the ensuing mêlée. The Japanese fighter went spinning down and Dupouy struggled back to base with four feet of wing missing. He walked away from his P-40 with only a few bruises, but the fighter was a complete write-off.

The Japanese had taken a hammering, and the blow to their pride became apparent when, the following day, Tokyo Radio announced that if the A V G pilots at Rangoon persisted in their 'unorthodox tactics', they would be treated as guerillas and shown no mercy when they fell into enemy hands. It was clear that from now on the Japanese would show a great deal more caution when penetrating Burmese airspace. The P-40s, with their distinctive sharks' teeth nose markings, were opponents to be treated very seriously.

On 28 December, the Japanese dispatched a small force of fifteen bombers towards Rangoon. Ten P-40s were sent off to intercept them, but as soon as the fighters were sighted the enemy turned tail and fled. The P-40 pilots chased them across southern Burma until they were forced to land through lack of fuel at Moulmein. Then, while the bombers made their escape and the P-40s refuelled, the Japanese put the second part of their plan into operation. Ten more bombers, escorted by twenty Zeros, swept down on Mingaladon. Four P-40s and ten Buffaloes intercepted the enemy force forty miles south-east of Rangoon, but they were beaten off by the fighter escort and the bombers roared over the airfield at three thousand feet, their bombs showering down to cause considerable damage to hangars, fuel dumps and grounded aircraft.

The Japanese returned the following day, and this time Rangoon itself was the target. Severe damage was inflicted on the railway station and the docks area, where large quantities of lend-lease equipment destined for China went up in flames. It seemed that the dwindling Allied fighter force was growing ever more powerless to stem the enemy's air onslaught.

The AVG, therefore, decided to carry the war to the enemy. Early in January three flights of P-40s, under the command of Squadron Leader Jack Newkirk, moved forward to the airstrip at Moulmein, just within range of the enemy airfield at Raheng in Thailand. On 3 January, Newkirk led six P-40s in a strafing attack on the Japanese base. Two enemy fighters were in the circuit when the Americans arrived overhead like thunderbolts; both were shot down before their pilots had a chance to take evasive action. Leaving four P-40s as top cover, Newkirk and his wingman, David L. ('Tex') Hill, dived on a line of parked enemy machines and raked them from end to end, leaving six of them in flames. Turning steeply, the P-40s came back again, howling across the field at twenty feet and sending streams of bullets into the installations. Japanese soldiers fired at them fruitlessly with rifles. Then the Americans were gone, speeding back across the Burmese border.

Further attacks on Japanese airfields in Thailand were mounted during January, but because of the range problem their damaging effect was strictly limited and they were more of a nuisance to the enemy than a serious threat. Then on 20 January 1942 the whole situation underwent a dramatic change. On that day, Japanese forces crossed the Thai border and advanced rapidly into southern Burma, pushing on towards Rangoon and overwhelming inferior numbers of British, Burmese and Indian troops.

From now on, for the allied air squadrons in Burma, it was to be a story of endless retreat. The RAF had at last begun to receive a few Hawker Hurricanes to supplement their obsolete

Fighter!

Buffaloes, but never more than thirty saw action and this number had been halved by the middle of February. It was left to the AVG to bear the brunt of the fighting. Fortunately, AVG pilot losses were few; but losses inevitably occurred, and some were made all the more tragic by the fact that they happened accidentally, rather than as a result of enemy action. On 7 February 1942 the AVG lost one of its finest pilots this way when Squadron Leader Robert Sandell – whose 1st Pursuit Squadron had moved south to Mingaladon – was killed while carrying out an air test in a newly-repaired P-40. What actually happened is not clear, but eyewitnesses told how the fighter appeared to enter a roll at low altitude and dive into the ground. Small, quietly-spoken Sandell was killed instantly. He was one of the AVG's first aces, with $5\frac{1}{4}$ enemy aircraft to his credit.

Sandell's place was taken by Squadron Leader Robert H. Neale, whose first, unenviable task was to lay plans for the eventual evacuation of the AVG from the Rangoon area, a move that now seemed inevitable. Before that happened, however, the AVG showed that it still had plenty of fight left. On 25 February, when forty Japanese bombers escorted by twenty Zeros headed for Rangoon, Bob Neale and six other pilots were waiting for them, their Tomahawks poised up-sun and ideally placed to intercept. In the short, whirlwind air battle that followed, Neale personally destroyed four bombers and probably destroyed another; his pilots claimed another six enemy aircraft between them. Bob Neale went on to become the American Volunteer Group's top-scoring pilot, with sixteen confirmed victories.

Early in March, with the Japanese at the gates of Rangoon, the AVG moved north to a new location, Magwe airfield, some two hundred miles away. From this base, together with the remnants of the RAF, the Americans harassed the Japanese ground forces as they advanced along the Sittang and Irrawaddy rivers. One of these ground attack missions, on 24 March, cost Squadron Leader Jack Newkirk his life when his P-40 was hit by light anti-aircraft fire during a strafing attack at Cheing-Mai. Newkirk had been living on borrowed time for weeks; he was always to be found where the fighting was thickest, and often took on appalling odds with little apparent regard for his own survival. Only a few days earlier he had been chased forty miles out to sea by three Japanese fighters after running out of ammunition; he outflew his pursuers and got back to base, miraculously uninjured, with his instrument panel shattered, his tail unit shot to ribbons and his tyres in shreds. At the time of his death Newkirk was the AVG's top scorer, with 10½ victories.

The AVG's occupation of Magwe aerodrome was destined to be a short one. Between 21 and 27 March the Japanese used all their available bombers in Burma to carry out a series of devastating attacks on the troublesome base, forcing the allies to abandon it. The RAF pulled back across the Indian frontier and the AVG moved to advanced bases in China, from where the Americans provided air cover for the retreating Chinese armies and carried out armed reconnaissance missions. They also attacked and destroyed part of the northern Burma Road and several bridges over the Salween river, impeding a Japanese thrust from Burma into Yunnan.

The days of the AVG as a cohesive fighting force, in fact, were coming to an end. From April onwards, flights of P-40s were scattered on airstrips all over south-west China, so that the available aircraft could cover as broad a front as possible. Aircraft were now in desperately short supply, but because the AVG was not formally part of the United States armed forces Chennault's repeated requests for replacement P-40s and pilots from the Tenth Army Air Force Command in India were just as repeatedly turned down. The feeling of having been virtually abandoned, coupled with combat fatigue and the knowledge of the pilots that they would have to go on risking their lives in worn-out equipment, added up to growing disillusionment and a general drop in morale. By the end of April, morale was at such a low ebb that twenty-four pilots went to Chennault and offered their resignations. Using a mixture of threats and cajolery, he persuaded all but four to stay – but the spirit of the AVG was never the same afterwards.

Fighter!

Nevertheless, the pilots continued to carry out their missions with great courage. On 7 May, in response to an urgent appeal from Chiang Kai-shek, they carried out a series of effective strikes on enemy road and river traffic across the Salween, causing severe disruption among the enemy's spearhead force, the 56th Infantry Division. Similar attacks were carried out at the end of the month, extending into June, but they were the AVG's swan song. On 4 July 1942 the American Volunteer Group officially ceased to be an independent fighting unit and became part of the newly-activated China Air Task Force, under command of the Tenth Air Force. Command of the CATF devolved on Claire Chennault, who exchanged his Chinese uniform for an American one and was given the rank of brigadier-general.

The AVG pilots, who had held the fort in Burma for so long against impossible odds, scattered far and wide. Few of them elected to remain in China. Those who did formed the nucleus of the new 23rd Fighter Group, still flying war-weary P-40s. They included Charles Older, who later became CO of the 75th Fighter Squadron and whose final score was seventeen enemy aircraft confirmed, 'Tex' Hill, Ed Rector and Gil Bright, all of whom continued to fly as civilians until they were officially commissioned in the USAAF. The group was commanded by Colonel Robert L. Scott, Jnr., who had flown several missions with the AVG. Several other notable pilots joined the 23rd's team in July, including Albert J. 'Ajax' Baumler, who had flown in the Spanish Civil War, John Alison, who became one of the first American day fighter pilots to intercept and destroy bombers at night, and Bruce K. Holloway, who destroyed ten enemy aircraft while flying with the 23rd and who became the US Air Force Vice Chief of Staff in the 1960s.

Other former AVG pilots went on to carve out distinguished careers for themselves in other theatres. Foremost among them was Lieutenant-Colonel Gregory 'Pappy' Boyington, the leading United States Marine Corps ace with twenty-eight victories, whose F4U Corsairs of the famous VMF-214 'Black Sheep'

Squadron blazed a trail of destruction across the Pacific. Boyington scored six of his victories with the AVG. Then there was Colonel James H. Howard, who also destroyed six Japanese aircraft with the AVG and who went on to gain six more victories with the 354th Fighter Group, flying P-51 Mustang escort missions over Germany.

The record of the American Volunteer Group stands unique in the annals of air combat. In just over six months of continual operations, with never more than seventy-nine pilots and fifty-five P-40s available at any one time, the group positively destroyed 286 enemy aircraft, a record that has never been equalled. How many of their 'probables' failed to get home will never be known.

The cost to the Americans was twelve pilots, four of whom were never found. Their unknown, unmarked graves lie shrouded in the jungle of the land they strove so valiantly to defend.

7 Fighters over the Desert

For the crew of the lone Junkers 88 reconnaissance aircraft, it seemed hard to believe that far below, among the scrub and sandy hills of Tunisia, men were fighting and dying; hard to believe that Erwin Rommel's once-proud Afrika Korps, which had swept across Libya and into Egypt in triumph just a year earlier, was being crushed like a nut between General Montgomery's Eighth Army, on the advance continually since the victory of El Alamein, and the Anglo-American forces which had landed in North Africa in November 1942.

Now, four months later, the end was in sight for German aspirations in North Africa. While RAF torpedo-bomber squadrons on Malta – the gallant George Cross island, which the might of Axis air power had tried so hard to break – hammered the Afrika Korps' supply lines, British and American fighter squadrons roved the skies over Tripoli and Tunisia, hounding the remnants of the Luftwaffe to destruction.

The Junkers 88's crew probably never saw the lone Spitfire that came swooping like a hawk out of the white Mediterranean sun. Cannon shells raked the Junkers from wingtip to wingtip and it fell burning, trailing sheets of fuel from ruptured tanks, to explode among the foothills of Kasserine.

Jubilantly, Squadron Leader Stanislaw Skalski circled the spot and then turned for home. It was a far cry from those desperate September days of 1939, when the smoke of Warsaw's burning had filled the cockpit of his little P-11 fighter . . .

Fighter!

Skalski had enjoyed a hectic career since his arrival in the United Kingdom in January 1940. As a member of No. 501 Squadron, RAF, he had fought his way through the Battle of Britain, destroying four enemy aircraft and damaging two more before being shot down and wounded on 5 September 1940. In the summer of 1941, flying with No. 306 (Polish) Squadron, he destroyed four Messerschmitt 109s before becoming an instructor for six months. He claimed two Focke-Wulf 190s and damaged a Bf 109 in the spring of 1942, and was then appointed to command No. 317 Squadron. He arrived in North Africa early the following year, leading a unit of experienced pilots known as the Polish Fighting Team – or, more popularly, as ' Skalski's Circus'. Flying Spitfire Mk. 9s – the first unit to do so in North Africa – the Poles were attached to No. 145 Squadron, RAF, and in eight weeks of operations their exploits became legendary. During that two-month period, they shot down more enemy aircraft than any other Polish fighter unit in 1943, and the pilots achieved such reputations that they were subsequently offered posts as commanding officers of other RAF fighter squadrons. Skalski, who shot down two Bf 109s as well as the Junkers 88 over Tunisia, became the first Pole to command an RAF fighter squadron, the famous No. 601. Later, in 1944, he was promoted to wing commander and led No. 2 (Polish) Wing for the rest of his operational career, flying Mustangs. He ended the war with a score of nineteen enemy aircraft destroyed, four of them over Poland in 1939.

Poor Skalski. In 1946 he returned to his homeland, only to find himself imprisoned for a time by the Russians, like so many of his countrymen who had fought alongside the British and Americans. Freedom, for the Poles, was a hard-won ideal.

North Africa, in the spring of 1943, was a killing-ground for allied fighter pilots. It had been a different story eighteen months earlier, when forty Commonwealth fighter squadrons, equipped mostly with Hawker Hurricanes and Curtiss P-40 Kittyhawks, had been unable to wrest air superiority from the Germans and Italians. The main opposition, then, had been the Messerschmitt

109s of the elite Jagdgeschwader 27, which included in its ranks one of the most famous German fighter aces of all time: Hans-Jochen Marseille. Not until the closing months of 1942 did the allies begin to achieve decisive victories in the air over the desert, and even then the Luftwaffe was defeated not in the air, but on the ground.

On 9 October 1942, for example, two weeks before the start of the Eighth Army's decisive counter-offensive at El Alamein, three squadrons of P-40s – Nos. 3, 112 and 450 (RAAF) – carried out a devastating low-level attack on enemy airfields in the vicinity of Daba, some ten minutes' flying time away from the Alamein defensive positions, where Intelligence had reported large numbers of German fighters bogged down in mud. It was just the opportunity the Desert Air Force had been awaiting. Thirty-two Kittyhawks swept down on Daba in the wake of a medium-level bombing attack by Martin Baltimores, and in the space of a few minutes they knocked out thirty Messerschmitt 109s. The Luftwaffe loss, which could not readily be made good, contributed in no small measure to the subsequent Commonwealth fighter superiority over the El Alamein front.

The desert battles of 1942 saw the increasing applications of both the Hurricane and Kittyhawk to ground attack work, for which the latter aircraft was particularly suited. The Kittyhawk's armament of six .5-inch machine-guns proved excellent for strafing and the aircraft was an adequate gun platform. It could also carry one 500-lb and two 250-lb bombs, and – at a pinch, for short-range missions – three 1,000-pounders. The Hurricanes, on the other hand, specialized more and more in the anti-tank role; No. 6 Squadron were the pioneers in this field, their Hurricane IIDs, armed with two 40mm cannon, going into action with deadly effect during the battle for the Gazala Line in June 1942. By the end of the month, the Hurricanes had destroyed twenty-six tanks, thirty-one armoured troop carriers, and many trucks, fuel bowsers and other soft-skinned targets.

In the latter half of 1942, therefore, the whole of the Desert Air Force was geared up to work in close co-operation with the

D

Fighter!

Eighth Army, its duties ranging from the provision of air cover over the front line to the protection of supply bases at the rear. In the latter respect, one of the most active squadrons was No. 73, whose Hurricanes were entrusted with the defence of Cairo during the late summer and autumn of 1942. During July, No. 73's pilots shot down twenty-three enemy aircraft between Suez and El Alamein for the loss of six of their own fighters.

By this time, growing numbers of Spitfires were reaching North Africa. The first Desert Air Force Spitfire squadron, No. 145, went into action on 1 June 1942, providing top cover for Hurricanes on a ground attack mission, but in fact Spitfires had first fired their guns in anger over Egypt several weeks earlier. For some time, the Germans had been using four high-flying Junkers Ju 86P-2 photo-reconnaissance aircraft to keep a watch on the British bases in the Suez Canal area. Every day, regular as clockwork, one would appear over Port Said and fly the whole length of the Suez Canal at 40,000 feet, its crew secure in their pressurized cabin, completely immune from both anti-aircraft fire and the Hurricanes which were responsible for defending the sector. Even when the first Spitfire Vc fighters arrived in Egypt early in May, the Germans could not have seriously considered them as a threat to their reconnaissance activities, for the Spitfire Vc's ceiling was only about 33,000 feet.

Three test pilots at the Aboukir Aircraft Depot, however, were determined that something ought to be done about the Ju-86 nuisance. They were Flying Officer G. W. H. Reynolds and Pilot Officers A. Gold and G. E. Genders, all of them veterans and among the most experienced fliers in the Middle East. With the help of the depot's technical staff, they set about stripping down one of the Spitfires, cutting out all extra weight such as armour plating. A new four-blade Rotol propeller was fitted, and the Spitfire's Merlin 46 engine specially modified to give more power at high altitude.

After several abortive attempts, it was Reynolds who made the first interception during the last week of May. He sighted a Ju 86 a few miles north of Cairo, flying at 37,000 feet, and went

94

in pursuit. The Germans saw him and climbed in an effort to escape, but Reynolds – frozen stiff and with his senses reeling – clung doggedly to the Junkers' tail and levelled out behind it at 42,000 feet, opening fire with the Spitfire's two specially-fitted .5 Browning machine-guns. His aim was good and the Junkers fell away in a diving turn, smoke streaming from one engine. Then thirty-eight-year-old Reynolds, utterly exhausted, blacked out and the Spitfire went out of control. He came to ten thousand feet lower down, regaining control and landing safely with only five gallons of petrol in his tank. Later, he learned that the Junkers had made a forced landing in the desert and that the crew had been taken prisoner.

A few days later, it was Genders' turn to score. Since the stripped-down Spitfire carried no radio, he flew in company with a standard Spitfire Vc whose job was to act as a marker aircraft. If Genders succeeded in damaging the Ju 86, the marker – flying several thousand feet lower down, but always in sight of Genders' aircraft – would hopefuly be able to finish off the enemy machine.

The Junkers was duly sighted, right on time as usual, and Genders managed to catch it at 45,000 feet a long way out to sea. He fired most of his ammunition at it and had the satisfaction of seeing it start to go down – it was subsequently destroyed, as planned, by the marker Spitfire – but he ran out of fuel shortly after turning back towards Aboukir. At 1,000 feet, still far out over the Mediterranean, Genders baled out. He had no dinghy – that, too, had been left behind to save weight – and so, with only his Mae West lifejacket for support, he started swimming in the general direction of Egypt. Twenty-two hours later, half dead with fatigue, he crawled ashore and, after a short rest, set out to thumb a lift back to Aboukir.

After a delay of over a week while a second Spitfire was stripped down, the Aboukir test pilots scored their third victory. It was Reynolds' turn once again, and on this occasion the chase took him to 50,000 feet, a record height for 1942. The whole flight proved agonizing, for the temperature in the cockpit was

Fighter!

67 degrees below zero and Reynolds, who was wearing the minimum of flying clothing, suffered severe pain and was partially paralysed. Nevertheless, he caught the Junkers 86 eight miles out to sea and shot it down. After that, there were no more high-level reconnaissance flights over the Suez Canal.

By the time the Eighth Army began to roll back the Afrika Korps and their supporting Italian divisions at El Alamein in October 1942, the Commonwealth fighter squadrons – joined now by two American units, the 57th and 79th Fighter Groups, both flying P-40s – had achieved a definite margin of air superiority over the battlefront. When German fighters appeared, however, they fought hard, despite the considerable odds against them. One 57th Fighter Group pilot, Captain Roy E. Whittaker, later wrote: 'The tough missions were bomber escorts to El Alamein against really excellent German pilots and aircraft in October of 1942. These battles were often so well executed by German pilots that many times we couldn't even get a shot in against their well-coordinated attacks. This was also true in December at the Mareth Line position, west of Benghazi.'

It was clear that the Luftwaffe still had plenty of fight left in it; but there was no escaping the fact that the German fighters were powerless to prevent the wholesale slaughter wrought on the Axis convoys by the Desert Air Force as Rommel's forces began the long retreat back through Cyrenaica. Meanwhile, further west, events were about to unfold which, ultimately, would render the Italian and German position in North Africa utterly hopeless.

On 8 November, Anglo-American forces carried out a series of simultaneous landings in Morocco and western Algeria. Operation Torch, as the landings were code-named, was the first large-scale amphibious operation to be undertaken by the allies, and was supported by seven British and four American aircraft carriers. Covering the landings were five squadrons of us Navy Grumman Wildcat fighters, nimble little aircraft which had already made their mark in the Pacific War; four squadrons of Supermarine Seafires – the naval version of the Spitfire, making its combat debut – five squadrons of Sea Hurricanes, three

96

squadrons of Grumman Martlets, as the Wildcat was known in Royal Navy service, and three squadrons of Fairey Fulmars.

The naval fighters had to contend not only with the Luftwaffe, but with the Vichy French fighter squadrons based in North Africa. Many of their pilots had fought through the Battle of France in 1940, and escaped across the Mediterranean; now, tragically, they were to be thrown into action against their former allies. Already, on 7 November, as the allied naval task force entered the Mediterranean, Martlets of No. 888 Squadron, Fleet Air Arm, had been launched from the carrier HMS *Formidable* to intercept and destroy a French Potez 63 reconnaissance aircraft which had flown over the armada at 10,000 feet.

The first series of air strikes launched by the allied carrier force, at first light on 8 November, caught the majority of the Vichy French squadrons on the ground and inflicted heavy losses on them. Some, however, escaped relatively intact and fought back hard. Among them was Groupe de Chasse I/5, whose Curtiss Hawks had carved such a reputation for themselves in the embattled sky over the Maginot Line before France's collapse in June 1940.

GC I/5's first task was to provide fighter escort for French bombers attacking the American beachhead at Fedala. The French fighter pilots had orders to fight only if attacked, and in fact showed a marked reluctance to engage the American Wildcats which intercepted the bombers over the beaches. It soon became apparent, however, that the Americans were taking no chances; the Wildcats swarmed all over the time-weary Hawks and shot four of them down.

The Hawks of GC II/5 fared even worse. Soon after dawn on the eighth, they took off to intercept waves of Douglas Dauntless dive-bombers which, with strong fighter escort, were attacking airfields in the vicinity of Casablanca. The French pilots had been told that the attackers were British, and it was with some astonishment that they saw the white stars stamped on their opponents' wings. But it was a case of kill or be killed, and the pilots of II/5 threw themselves into the fight with the same fervour they had shown over their homeland eighteen months earlier. They destroyed three Wildcats, but the Hawks proved incapable of absorbing punishment from the Americans' .5-inch machine-guns and five of them plunged to the ground in flames. Among the dead French pilots was Commandant Tricaud, who had been shot down three times without injury during the Battle of France.

At the end of the day, the Americans had lost seven Wildcats and the French ten Curtiss Hawks. Together with the losses sustained on the ground, it marked the end of the Hawk's operational career with the French Air Force.

French Dewoitine D.520 fighters also challenged the allies on several occasions, but they too proved no match for the British and American fighters. On the morning of the eighth, the British Seafires scored their first victory when Lieutenant G. C. Baldwin shot down a D.520, and five more Dewoitines were destroyed by the Sea Hurricanes of No. 800 Squadron. The Americans also came into contact with D.520s when, on the ninth, the 31st Fighter Group – flying Spitfires from Gibraltar – were asked to provide air cover for US ground forces approaching the airfield of Tafaraoui, Oran. As they approached their objective the Americans, flying through scattered showers, sighted what they took to be four Hurricanes orbiting the airfield; the Hurricanes, however, turned out to be D.520s, and these shot down one of the Spitfires. The remaining four Spits, led by Major Harrison Thyng, fell on the Vichy fighters and destroyed three of them, leaving the sole survivor to flee for home. One of the D.520s was shot down by Thyng; it was the start of a combat career that was to end in the cockpit of an F-86 Sabre over Korea, where he destroyed five Russian MiG-15 jets.

Once the Vichy French airfields in Algeria had been secured, the build-up of allied fighter squadrons proceeded at a fast rate. The first allied fighter unit to be based on Algerian soil was No. 43 Squadron RAF, whose Hurricanes touched down at Maison Blanche, near Algiers, less than an hour after the field had been captured by an American combat team. They were soon followed by the Spitfires of Nos. 81 and 242 Squadrons. Other units arriving in North Africa that day were Nos. 72, 93, 111 and 152 Squadrons with Spitfires, No. 225 with Hurricanes and No. 255 with Beaufighters. On the American side, the earliest arrivals were the Spitfires of the 31st and 52nd Fighter Groups, followed by the P-40s of the 33rd Fighter Group, the 1st and 14th Fighter Groups with P-38 Lightnings, and the 81st and 350th Fighter Groups with P-39D Airacobras.

It was not until the evening of 8 November that the Luftwaffe made a serious attempt to interfere wih the allied landings. At about 17.00, the Seafires of No. 807 Squadron had just taken off from HMS *Furious* when fifteen Junkers 88s appeared out of the gathering dusk and dive-bombed the carrier, scoring one hit and several near misses. There were several more raids during the course of the operations, but they usually took the form of aircraft flying over the fleet in small numbers at high altitude, dropping their bombs ineffectively and escaping before the defending fighters could get to grips with them. One Heinkel 111 was, however, shot down by the Martlets of 882 Squadron on the ninth, followed by a Junkers 88 destroyed by 888 Squadron on the tenth. That same evening, a formation of twenty Junkers 88s was intercepted by a mixed fighter force from Maison Blanche, including the Hurricanes of 43 Squadron, and in a twenty-minute running fight the enemy lost eleven bombers.

As the allies began their advance, the lack of suitable forward airstrips became a serious problem. Existing airfields became overcrowded, and their ever-increasing distance from the front line meant that fighters could spend only ten minutes, or even less, in the combat area. Early in December, in an attempt to remedy the situation, the Spitfires of No. 93 Squadron were sent forward to a muddy strip at Medjez el Bab, but they had barely arrived when Messerschmitt 109s swept down on them and shot them up.

A new challenge to allied air superiority had now arrived in North Africa in the shape of the first Focke-Wulf 190s, which operated as fighter-bombers under the control of Fliegerführer

Tunis and which, for some considerable time, enabled the Luftwaffe in Tunisia to hold its own against numerically superior forces. The Focke-Wulfs flew a prodigious number of sorties and became a real thorn in the allies' flesh, carrying out numerous low-level bombing attacks against allied ports and supply dumps as well as providing close support in defence of the last Axis stronghold. It was mainly to counter the threat of the Focke-Wulfs that Spitfire Mk. 9s were hurriedly shipped out to North Africa, serving first with Stanislaw Skalski's Polish Fighting Team and then, from February 1943, with No. 72 Squadron.

On 7 April 1943, following desperate fighting, the American II Corps linked up with the British Eighth Army and the drive northwards into Tunisia began. At the same time, the allied air forces began an all-out campaign to destroy the remnants of the Luftwaffe in North Africa; they also launched a series of heavy attacks on enemy airfields in Sicily and southern Italy, where the enemy was assembling fleets of transport aircraft – Junkers 52s and massive, six-engined Messerschmitt Me 323 'Giants' – in a frantic attempt to get supplies and reinforcements through to the Afrika Korps.

Some enemy transports managed to slip across the Mediterranean under cover of darkness. When they came by day, however, they were shot down like flies by the allied fighters. They suffered their worst losses on 18 April 1943, when the Luftwaffe scraped together all the transport aircraft it could muster and threw them over the Mediterranean in one huge formation, laden with troops and equipment.

On that brilliant Palm Sunday afternoon, long lines of battle-ready German troops, fresh from training camps in Italy, filed aboard ninety big three-engined Junkers 52s that stood waiting on their Sicilian airfields. There were 1,800 soldiers in all, twenty to each aircraft. At 16.30 the armada took off and set course south-westwards, flying in three immaculate 'Vs' and keeping low over the sea to avoid detection by radar stations on Malta. With the transports came the fighter escort, thirty Messerschmitt 109s and 110s, as well as a few Italian Macchi 202s.

Three hundred miles away, on the other side of the Mediterranean, while the stream of German aircraft took off amid clouds of dust, the air also thundered with the sound of engines as the forty-eight P-40 Warhawks of the USAAF's 57th and 324th Fighter Groups lifted away from their desert airfield of El Djem. Climbing steadily, they flew northwards along the Tunisian coast. The pilots' orders were to patrol the Cape Bon area and the Gulf of Tunis. Over Sousse, halfway to the Gulf, twelve sleek aircraft came up from the east and slipped into position above the American formation, at 15,000 feet. They were the Spitfires of No. 92 Squadron, RAF.

The big fighter formation reached Cape Bon and began its patrol. For ninety minutes the pilots flew back and forth over the sea, the squadrons wheeling lazily in the sky at heights of between 7,000 and 15,000 feet. By 18.00 hours, the sun was a great orange ball in the west and it was becoming increasingly difficult to see.

In the cockpit of one of the 57th Fighter Group P-40s, Captain Roy Whittaker gazed through the perspex, narrowing his eyes as he searched the western sky through the glare of the sinking sun. There was nothing: the allied fighters seemed to have the sky to themselves. Like most of the other pilots, Whittaker was tired and bored after long, cramped hours in the air. They had already flown one lengthy patrol that day without sighting an enemy aircraft, and now, with only minutes to go before they were due to return to base, it seemed as though they were going to be out of luck yet again.

Suddenly, something caught Whittaker's eye: the flash of sunlight on a wing, low over the sea. A moment later, he made out a large formation of enemy fighters, weaving from side to side over the glittering water. But it was not the fighters that made Whittaker open his eyes wide in disbelief. Behind them, like a massive flight of geese, Junkers 52 transports stretched as far as the eye could see. They were flying in perfect formation as though at an air show, heading in towards the Tunisian coast. It was a fighter pilot's dream.

101

Fighter!

While twelve P-40s and the Spitfires of 92 Squadron went for the enemy fighter escort, the remaining thirty-six P-40s tumbled like an avalanche on the Junkers. Roy Whittaker swept down on the leading formation and fired at a pair of transports, seeing pieces fly off one of them, then he climbed and circled for another attack. This time he was more successful; two Junkers went down in flames and a few moments later they were joined by a third. Pulling up sharply, Whittaker found the grey belly of a Messerschmitt 109 filling his sights. He fired, and the enemy fighter spun into the sea. Whittaker glanced at his watch. He had destroyed four enemy aircraft in three minutes.

Everywhere it was the same story. Young pilots for whom this was the first taste of combat suddenly found themselves turned into aces in a matter of minutes as one transport after the other went down before their guns. Lieutenants Arthur B. Cleaveland and Richard E. Duffy destroyed five Junkers apiece, while another 57th Group pilot, Lieutenant MacArthur Powers, shot down four Ju 52s and a Messerschmitt 109.

As they bored in again and again, the fighter pilots began to run into a storm of small-arms fire from the transports. Hatches and doors were frantically jettisoned and the German troops crouched in the slipstream, blazing away at the attackers with rifles and light machine-guns. More than one Warhawk pilot was sickened as he watched his bullets churn the inside of a Junkers' fuselage into a bloody shambles.

Deprived of their fighter cover, by this time scattered all over the sky by the Spitfires and Warhawks, the slow transports had no chance. Many of the Junkers pilots who escaped the initial onslaught pushed down the noses of their aircraft and headed for the coast at full throttle, intent on making a forced landing on the beach – only to be pursued and caught by the much faster fighters and sent blazing into the surf.

Some were lucky, but only because shortage of fuel compelled the allied pilots to abandon the chase. Behind them, as they turned for home, the fighters left a nightmare scene of carnage in the lurid glare of the setting sun; patches of oil and wreckage drifting on the water, with a handful of survivors struggling among them; tall columns of smoke rising from the crashed aircraft that littered the coast.

In just ten minutes, for the loss of six of their own number, the allied fighters had destroyed seventy-seven enemy aircraft – more than the RAF had shot down during the worst day's fighting of the Battle of Britain. Fifty-nine of those aircraft were Junkers transports, and with them a thousand picked men of the Afrika Korps went to their deaths. So ended the great air battle that was to go down in history as the Palm Sunday Massacre.

Four days later the Germans tried again, this time with huge Messerschmitt 323s. Sixteen aircraft, all from Transport-Geschwader 5 and fully laden with desperately-needed supplies of fuel, were heading for Tunis with a small fighter escort when they were caught off Cape Bon by two squadrons of RAF Spitfires and four squadrons of South African Air Force P-40s. In five minutes, the fighters shot down fourteen of the mighty transports and seven of their escorting fighters, leaving the coastal waters aflame with burning petrol. Two hundred and forty tons of fuel never reached the Afrika Korps that day, and of the 140 air-crew of TG 5 who took part in the operation, only nineteen survived.

For the Afrika Korps, it was the end. Yet right up to the last, the Germans persisted in their reckless attempts to fling reinforcements into the cauldron of Tunisia. The few who did get through were sacrificed on the battlefield or marched into captivity when the final offensive rolled over them in May.

8 Escort Fighter

Like an avalanche, the enemy fighters came tumbling out of the sun. There were thirty-six of them, twin-engined Messerschmitt 110s, arrowing down towards the B-17 Flying Fortresses that spun their contrails twenty-five thousand feet over Germany. The American gunners crouched behind their weapons and watched as the glittering crosses grew rapidly bigger in their sights. They knew that they would be lucky to weather this new onslaught, for between them and the cannon of the Germans stood just one friendly fighter – a P-51 Mustang, weaving watchfully overhead.

It was 11 January 1944. That morning, several groups of US 8th Air Force B-17s had droned in over the north German coast on course for their target at Oschersleben, deep in the heart of the Reich, shepherded by the long-range Mustangs of the USAAF's 354th Fighter Group. Squadrons of Focke-Wulfs and Messerschmitts had hit the bombers over the coast and had gone on attacking right up to the target area. By the time Oschersleben was reached the bomber groups had become dislocated and the escorting Mustangs scattered all over the sky.

Then, as one of the B-17 groups unloaded its bombs on the target and turned for home, the German fighters came boring in yet again. From the cockpit of the lone 354th Group Mustang, Major James H. Howard saw them coming and immediately turned to meet them head-on. Jim Howard had learned his trade the hard way, flying with the American Volunteer Group in

Burma. He was going to need all his skill to come out of this battle in one piece. The Messerschmitts broke in all directions as Howard ripped in among them. A 110 shot across his nose and he raked it with his four .50 machine-guns; the fighter blew up, its debris fluttering from a spreading cloud of smoke.

The Germans formed up for a second attempt and once again Howard broke them up, sending another fighter down in flames. It was only the beginning. Three more times the enemy attacked, and three times Howard fought them off single-handed. During the two final attacks, only one of the Mustang's guns was working – but Howard managed to destroy a third enemy fighter and damage at least three more.

Suddenly the sky was empty. Probably short of fuel, the Luftwaffe pilots broke off the action and headed for home. With Howard still escorting them, the battle-scarred B-17s set course for England.

For his exploit, Major Howard later received the Congressional Medal of Honour. He was the only British-based American fighter pilot to win the highest US decoration for valour during the Second World War. It was a tribute not only to his superb flying skill, but to the splendid qualities of the little fighter he flew. Yet again, the Mustang had proved that it was a match for anything in the skies of Europe. And this was the aeroplane whose life had begun four years earlier as a rough sketch on a piece of paper in a London hotel room . . .

At the beginning of 1940, Britain had turned to the United States in a search for a fast, heavily-armed fighter aircraft capable of operating effectively at heights of over 20,000 feet. The Royal Air Force had an urgent requirement for this type of machine to supplement the Hurricanes and Spitfires which were then being turned out at maximum rate by the British aircraft industry. The problem was that the latter could not cope with the RAF's plans for rapid expansion; although the re-equipment of British-based fighter squadrons with Spitfires and Hurricanes was almost complete by January 1940, it would be some time before production could proceed rapidly enough to meet the demands of the fighter squadrons based overseas – squadrons which, in the meantime, had to soldier on with obsolescent equipment.

At first sight, the American market seemed disappointing. The best US fighter aircraft then in operational service – the Curtiss P-40 – fell a long way short of measuring up to the RAF's requirement, and two more American fighter designs that looked promising – the P-38 and P-39 – would not be ready for service until the spring of 1941. The RAF's need, however, was pressing, and it was decided to order a number of P-40s. Since the Curtiss production line was already fully occupied in meeting the demands of the US Army Air Corps, the British Direct Purchase Commission approached another American manufacturer, North American Aircraft Inc. of Los Angeles, and asked them if they would be willing to build a variant of the P-40 for the RAF under sub-contract.

North American were reluctant to take on sub-contract work. Instead, they offered to design and build a completely new aircraft to meet the RAF's requirement. The Air Ministry agreed, and a North American delegation headed by J. H. 'Dutch' Kindelberger and J. L. Atwood, president and vice-president of the company, visited Britain to discuss details. In an hotel room early in February, with the London fog swirling outside, they pored over the Air Ministry specification and Kindelberger swiftly drew a few lines on a scrap of paper. The resulting sketch showed a clean, long-wing monoplane with an in-line engine and square-cut wings and tail : the Mustang was born.

The Air Ministry's time limit for completion of a prototype was 120 days. North American did it in 117. Work on the prototype – designated NA-73 by the manufacturer – was started in April 1940 and the aircraft, minus its engine, was rolled out in August. A number of modifications were carried out before the machine made its maiden flight on 26 October, powered by an Allison V-1710-39 engine developing 1,100 hp. Even before the prototype flew, the British Direct Purchase Commission had placed an order for 320 Mustang Is, as the aircraft was to be known in RAF service.

The first production Mustang I flew on 1 May 1941, and the second machine arrived in Britain for handling trials the following October. RAF test pilots at Boscombe Down found that the aircraft performed well up to 15,000 feet, where a maximum speed of 380 mph was achieved, but performance was drastically reduced above 20,000 feet and at 25,000 feet the Mustang was generally outclassed by the Spitfire V. As a low and medium altitude fighter, however, the Mustang showed excellent qualities. It was faster than the Spitfire in a dive, and recovered without difficulty from speeds as high as 500 mph.

Because of its limitations as a high-altitude interceptor, it was decided to use the Mustang as a high-speed ground attack and tactical reconnaissance fighter, and it was in this role that it entered service with Army Co-operation Command in July 1942. An F24 camera was installed aft of the cockpit on the port side of the rear fuselage, and armament consisted of two fixed .50 machine-guns fitted below the engine and two .30 and one .50 guns mounted in each wing. The Mustang's first operational mission, a cross-Channel sweep, was flown on 27 July 1942, and soon afterwards the aircraft were engaged in photographing the Dieppe area in preparation for the big allied raid of 19 August. During this operation, four RAF Mustang squadrons carried out seventy-two low-level reconnaissance sorties over the beachhead.

Meanwhile, following an almost complete lack of interest in the Mustang during the early stages of its development, the USAAF had at last begun to wake up to the aircraft's potential and had ordered two early production Mustang Is for evaluation under the designation P-51. These aircraft were fitted with an improved Allison engine rated at 1,125 hp at 15,000 feet, and the armament was changed to four wing-mounted 20mm cannon. One hundred and fifty P-51s were ordered for the RAF with the designation Mustang IA, but fifty-five of them were repossessed by the USAF. Their fuselage tanks were removed and replaced by two cameras, and the aircraft were re-designated F-6A.

Two more aircraft in this batch were also retained by the USAAF for engine development, and were fitted with Packard-built Rolls-Royce Merlin 61 engines. Four British Mustangs were also converted by Rolls-Royce. The increase in performance was dramatic, maximum speed being raised to 441 mph. Production of the Merlin-powered P-51B got under way in the autumn of 1942 at North American's Inglewood factory.

Before the Merlin-powered variant came along, however, the USAAF had ordered two more Mustang versions equipped with up-rated Allison engines. The first of these was the A-36A, a ground attack variant fitted with a V-1710-87 Allison motor. It was armed with six .50 machine-guns, two under the engine and four in the wings, and could carry two 500-pound bombs. Five hundred A-36As were produced for the USAAF.

The second variant was the P-51A, powered by a 1,200-hp V-1710-81 engine which gave it a top speed of 390 mph. Armament was four wing-mounted .50 guns, and the aircraft could carry either a pair of 500-pound bombs or drop-tanks. Three hundred and ten were built for the USAAF and the RAF received fifty. Thirty-five more were converted to the low-level reconnaissance role and designated F-6B.

For a short time, the A-36A and the P-51A were known as 'Invader' and 'Apache' in USAAF service before the name Mustang was adopted for all variants. The A-36A was the first Mustang variant to see operational service with the USAAF, participating in the allied invasion of Sicily in July 1943. The following September the 23rd and 51st Fighter Groups of the 14th Air Force, operating in the China-Burma-India theatre, also re-equipped with Mustangs; these were P-51Bs and P-51Cs, the first of the many variants fitted with Packard-Merlin engines.

In November 1943, the first USAAF Mustang unit arrived in Britain – the 354th Fighter Group. Based at Boxted, near Colchester, the group initially came under the command of the 9th Air Force. On 1 December the group's P-51Bs took off on their first operational mission – a sweep over Belgium and the Pas de Calais. The twenty-three pilots who took part were led by Lt-Col Don Blakeslee of the Debden-based 4th Fighter Group, flying a P-47 Thunderbolt. On 5 December the 354th – now under the operational control of the 8th Air Force – flew the first P-51 escort mission to Amiens, but the Luftwaffe failed to appear and the Mustang pilots returned to base without having fired their guns in anger.

On 13 December the 354th flew the longest fighter mission of the war up to that date when the Mustangs – together with P-38 Lightnings of the 55th Fighter Group – escorted B-17s to Kiel and back, a round trip of 1,000 miles. Three days later, on the sixteenth, the Mustangs once again penetrated deep into Germany on an escort mission to Bremen, and it was on this raid that the group's first enemy aircraft, a Bf. 110, was destroyed by Lt Charles F. Gumm of the 355th Squadron. This success was marred by the loss on the return flight of Major Owen M. Seaman, the commander of the 353rd Squadron, who disappeared without trace over the North Sea.

By the end of the year the 354th had shot down eight enemy aircraft for the loss of eight Mustangs. It was a far from encouraging picture, and the pilots entered the new year determined to score more favourable results. Their big chance came on 5 January 1944, when they once again escorted B-17s to Kiel; the American formation was attacked by shoals of Messerschmitt 110s and Focke-Wulf 190s and a savage dogfight developed. When it ended, the Mustang pilots claimed the destruction of eighteen German aircraft for no loss. The Luftwaffe was also up in strength when the 354th escorted the Fortresses to Oschersleben on 11 January – the day that saw Major James Howard's one-sided battle against three dozen enemy fighters. On 11 February the 354th's Mustangs again fought their way through strong Luftwaffe opposition to Frankfurt, claiming fourteen enemy aircraft destroyed for the loss of two of their own number. One of the latter was flown by Colonel Kenneth R. Martin, the Group's CO, who collided with a Messerschmitt 110 but survived to spend the rest of the war in a prison camp. Command of the unit was assumed by the newly-promoted Lt-Col Howard, and during the last week of February he led the 354th on its longest penetration mission so far – a 1,100-mile round trip to Leipzig. During this raid, the Mustang pilots claimed another sixteen German aircraft destroyed.

Meanwhile, three other USAAF fighter groups in England had become operational on the Mustang during February. In the 9th Air Force, the 354th was joined by the 363rd Fighter Group on 22 February, while on 11 February the first Mustang Group within the 8th Air Force – the 357th – flew its first operational mission, a fighter sweep over Rouen. The 8th USAAF's second Mustang group was Don Blakeslee's 4th, which exchanged its P-47s for P-51s on 27 February. Less than 24 hours later, Blakeslee was leading the group into action on an escort mission over France; his pilots had less than one hour's flying time in the Mustang!

There was considerable rivalry between the Mustang and Thunderbolt fighter groups, and the fact that on more than one occasion Mustangs returned to base riddled with .50 bullet-holes after being mistaken for Messerschmitt 109s by trigger-happy Thunderbolt pilots served to intensify it.

The rivalry was particularly keen between the 354th and Hubert Zemke's 56th P-47 'Wolfpack' Fighter Group. In the summer of 1943, Zemke's pilots had claimed the destruction of 100 German aircraft in 86 days. Early in 1944 the 354th went all out to better this score, but on 21 February – their 83rd day of operations – the tally of the Mustang pilots stood at 92 enemy aircraft destroyed. By nightfall that same day, however, the 354th's score had risen to 103, and the following day twelve more enemy aircraft were claimed during an escort mission to Oschersleben.

By the end of February 1944, several of the 354th's pilots were aces with five or more enemy aircraft to their credit. Leading the field was Lt Charles F. Gumm, with seven confirmed victories. Tragically, he was killed on 1 March when the engine of his Mustang failed on take-off. Rather than bail out and abandon the aircraft to crash on the little village of Nayland, he stayed in the cockpit long enough to guide it towards open ground. By that time he was too low to jump, and his body was found by villagers near the burning wreckage.

On 6 March 1944 allied fighters appeared in the sky over Berlin for the first time when Don Blakeslee's 4th Fighter Group escorted B-17s to the German capital. The 4th's Mustangs returned to Berlin two days later and claimed sixteen enemy aircraft destroyed. During March alone, 'Blakeslee's Bachelors' claimed 156 German aircraft confirmed, together with 8 probables; 100 were claimed in just fifteen days, from 18 March to 1 April inclusive. The pilots of the 354th Fighter Group, meanwhile, were being earmarked more and more for tactical bombing missions – the first of which had been flown on 26 March, when the Mustangs dive-bombed the marshalling yards at Creil and plastered them with 500-pounders – and they had little hope of recapturing the lead which they had established the previous month. Blakeslee's red-nosed Mustangs were well out in front, and appeared to have every intention of staying there.

During the spring of 1944, several more Mustang groups became operational within the 8th Air Force: the 335th, 361st, 479th, 339th, 20th, 352nd and 359th. All these groups were equipped with P-51Bs or P-51Cs. The 9th Air Force's complement of two groups – the 354th and 363rd – remained unchanged. In June 1944, however, two tactical reconnaissance squadrons – the 12th and 15th, equipped with F-6B and F-6C Mustangs – were added to the 9th Air Force. Based on Chalgrove, near Oxford, these aircraft flew an intensive series of photo-reconnaissance missions in support of the allied armies in Normandy.

While the British-based P-51s of the 8th Air Force ranged deeply over France and Germany during the spring of 1944, other Mustang groups were proving their worth in the Mediterranean theatre. Four P-51B and C Mustang groups – the 52nd (12th Air Force) and the 31st, 332nd and 325th (15th Air Force)

– were operating in support of the allied offensive in Italy; one of them, the 31st, had been flying Spitfires until it converted to Mustangs in April. On 21 April the 31st Fighter Group mounted its first 'big show' with the new Mustangs when it was detailed to escort a B-24 mission raiding the Rumanian oil refineries at Ploeşti. The group's task was to meet the bombers after they had left the target area and shepherd them home. Near Bucharest, the Mustang Pilots sighted a formation of B-24s being attacked by at least sixty enemy fighters; attacking out of the sun, the Americans took the enemy completely by surprise and a savage dogfight sprang up. Two Mustangs went down in flames, but the 31st's pilots claimed seventeen enemy fighters destroyed, seven probably destroyed and ten damaged. It was a notable success that earned the group a distinguished unit citation.

On 22 July, the 31st Fighter Group was once again detailed for an escort mission to Ploeşti. While bomb-carrying P-38 Lightnings of the 82nd Group attacked the oil refinery installations, the Mustangs strafed a nearby airfield before going on to land at Piryatin in Russia. On 25 July, operating out of the Russian base, the group's thirty-five Mustangs escorted the P-38s on a ground attack mission to the German-held airfield at Mielec in Poland. During the return flight, they ran headlong into a formation of thirty-six Stukas, laden with bombs and heading for the Russian lines. The Mustangs ripped in among the slow-flying dive-bombers and a frightful slaughter ensued. Within minutes, the wreckage of twenty-seven Stukas was blazing on the ground. This destruction of an entire Luftwaffe dive-bomber wing earned the 31st Group its second distinguished unit citation. On 26 July, the Mustangs flew back to their base in Italy.

Meanwhile, the allied invasion of Normandy and the days that followed in June 1944 had been a hectic time for the Mustang groups of the 8th and 9th Air Forces, the pilots flying a spate of close-support missions and air patrols over the beaches. Early in July, the F-6 Mustangs of the 12th and 15th Tactical Reconnaissance Squadrons moved from Chalgrove to a temporary airstrip near Le Molay, where they stayed until the allied breakthrough at St Lo permitted another move on 11 August, this time to Rennes. During the closing months of the year the recce Mustang squadrons made two more moves, following in the wake of the allied armies as they pushed on towards Germany.

During June, the UK-based Mustangs accounted for a number of V-1 flying bombs. The 354th Group was particularly active; its new base at Lashenden, Kent was right in the path of the 'doodlebugs' as they sped on their way to London. On 18 June, Lt-Col Richard Turner destroyed two V-1s which he encountered while returning from a dive-bombing mission over France, and a few days later Lt Joe Powers got two more, sharing a third with another pilot.

The Americans' experience of dealing with jet-powered aircraft, however, was soon to be widened beyond shooting down pilotless V-1s. On 28 July 1944, the pilots of nine 8th Air Force P-51s escorting a B-17 wing 25,000 feet over Merseburg suddenly spotted several aircraft at 32,000 feet, approaching the American formation very rapidly and streaming dense contrails. The enemy – five Messerschmitt 163 rocket-propelled fighters – circled to make a head-on pass at the bombers, but altered course and headed for the Mustang escort when the latter turned to meet them. Before the American pilots had time to take any further action, the 163s had streaked below them at over 500 mph and were gone.

The Me 163s put in another appearance on 5 August 1944, and this time the Mustangs – escorting B-17s over Magdeburg – were not so lucky. From 35,000 feet the rocket fighters dived on the P-51s in line astern and opened fire with their 30mm cannon. The Mustangs scattered in all directions, but it was too late; three of their number were already spinning down in flames and the 163s had vanished before the other P-51 pilots realized what was happening. On 16 August, however, the Mustang pilots proved that the Luftwaffe's terrifying new weapon had not made the propeller-driven aircraft completely obsolete when a pair of P-51s destroyed two 163s which were attacking a straggling B-17.

In September 1944 the American daylight bomber formations began to encounter increasing numbers of a new German type : the twin-jet Messerschmitt 262. With its greater endurance and four 30mm cannon, the 262 was a far more formidable opponent than the rocket-powered Me 163, but even so it was by no means invincible. On 9 October, Mustangs destroyed two Me 262s near Achmer, where the Luftwaffe's first jet fighting wing was based. A Messerschmitt 163 was also shot down by Mustangs on that same day. In December, the P-51 pilots of the 31st Fighter Group scored the 15th Air Force's first jet victory when, on the twenty-second of that month, a 262 was shot down by Lts Eugene P. McGlauflin and Roy L. Scales during a photo-reconnaissance mission. The second time the 31st's Mustangs ran into the German jets was on 22 March 1945, when a lone 262 was destroyed by Captain William J. Dillard during an escort mission to Ruhland. Then, on 24 March, came a grand finale for the 15th AF when the 31st Fighter Group destroyed no fewer than five Me 262s while escorting heavy bombers to Berlin.

By the autumn of 1944, the majority of Mustang units in the European Theatre of Operations had re-equipped with the P-51D, the latest variant of the Mustang fitted with a transparent 'tear-drop' cockpit which gave the pilot excellent all-round vision. The P-51D was armed with six .50 machine-guns, and with two of these removed could carry two 1,000-pound bombs or up to ten five-inch rockets. Maximum speed was 437 mph at 15,000 feet; range was 2,300 miles with maximum fuel, and service ceiling was 41,900 feet. In the China-Burma-India theatre, however, the Mustang units of the 5th and 10th Air Forces still soldiered on with the P-51B and C, and it was while flying these variants that two Mustang pilots – Major John Herbst and Lt-Col Edward McComas – became the CBI's top-scoring US aces.

McComas's most fruitful day was 23 December 1944, when he shot down five Japanese fighters in the course of an hour.

115

Fighter!

While leading sixteen Mustangs of the 118th Tactical Reconnaissance Squadron back from an attack on the Wuchang-Hankow ferry terminals, he strafed a Japanese airfield at Wuchang, destroying two aircraft on the ground. As he climbed away, he spotted an Oscar fighter and attacked it from astern; his bullets struck home and the pilot baled out. Another enemy airfield, Ehur Tao Kow, lay on his route home and he decided to attack it too. Arriving overhead, he saw a pair of Oscars taking off and dived on them just as they got airborne. He fired on the leading aircraft and it flicked sharply to one side, colliding with the second fighter. Both Oscars crashed on the airfield boundary, burning fiercely. Pulling his Mustang round in a tight turn he came in behind two more Oscars and fired a long burst into each. They came apart like tissue paper and dived into the ground.

McComas, with fourteen victories, was narrowly beaten by Major John C. Herbst, known as 'Pappy' among the pilots of his group because at thirty-five he was a good ten years older than most of them. On 1 January 1945, Herbst's score stood at fifteen enemy aircraft destroyed. Then, on the sixteenth, he shot down two Japanese bombers and the following day he destroyed a Tojo fighter over Tachang, bringing his score up to eighteen.

When the Mustang had entered service in the CBI at the end of 1943 – employed principally in escorting B-24 heavy bombers raiding Japanese targets in Burma – the Americans had found themselves in possession of an aircraft which, for the first time, could meet the Zero on more than favourable terms and which was superior on every account to the most numerous Japanese Army fighter, the Oscar. Now, during the early months of 1945, the Mustang demonstrated its superiority in a dramatic way by becoming the first American fighter to take part in strikes against the Japanese home islands. The Mustangs involved were long-range P-51Ds of the 20th Air Force, operating from bases on Iwo Jima after the island was captured in February–March 1945.

It would be some months yet before the red sun of Japan finally sank below the horizon, but in Europe the war was drawing to its inevitable close. The air war during those final months was fought with incredible savagery as the Luftwaffe, still far from completely beaten, threw in everything it had in an attempt to stem the allied air onslaught. On 1 January 1945, hundreds of German fighter-bombers hurled themselves on the allied airfields in Holland, Belgium and northern France with the aim of paralysing the allied air forces on the ground, affording some respite to the hard-pressed German ground forces battling in the Ardennes. They very nearly succeeded; some three hundred British and American aircraft were knocked out in a matter of minutes, and very few allied units were airborne to oppose the attackers.

One of the units that was fortunate enough to be in the air was the 487th Fighter Squadron (352nd Fighter Group). The P-51Ds had just taken off from their base at Asch, in Belgium, on a routine patrol when they received reports of waves of enemy aircraft heading in their direction. Led by Lt-Col John C. Meyer, the Mustangs dived headlong into a formation of Focke-Wulf 190s and broke it up. Within seconds, a twisting dogfight developed over Asch. Captain William T. Whisner, leading one of the Mustang flights, looked back to find a 190 sitting on his tail and a moment later his P-51 shuddered as seven 20mm shells slammed into it. Whisner managed to shake off the pursuer and, despite the damage to his aircraft, destroyed no fewer than five 190s in the next few minutes. The other P-51 pilots claimed five more.

The 487th's commander, Lt-Col Meyer, had destroyed an Arado 234 jet bomber the previous day – one of the few allied pilots to shoot down an aircraft of this type. During the closing stages of the war the German jets became increasingly troublesome, but by this time the allied fighter pilots had evolved tactics to deal with them, either by maintaining standing patrols in the vicinity of the front line to catch the jets as they sneaked across at low level or by hanging around near the German airfields,

117

braving the murderous flak to shoot down the jets as they took off and landed.

The latter method was favoured by one Mustang ace of the 55th Fighter Group, Captain Donald M. Cummings. On 25 February 1945, he orbited the German airfield of Giebelstadt at a respectable altitude until he saw a 262 moving out to take off. Leaving the rest of his section to provide top cover, he went down in a steep dive and opened fire on the jet at a range of 1,000 yards. The 262 dug in a wingtip and exploded.

Cummings flew on to another German jet fighter base at Leipheim, where he surprised a second 262 about to land. Cautiously, the American closed in to 400 yards and waited until the unsuspecting 262 pilot dropped his landing gear before opening fire. Rolling over and over, the jet struck the ground and blew up.

During the last weeks of hostilities, the Mustang groups were employed more and more in the ground-attack role, operating from bases only a few miles behind the front line. One of the first Mustang units to be based on German soil was the 354th, which arrived at Ober Olm on 8 April 1945. A week later the group's P-51s attacked several enemy airfields in Czechoslovakia, one squadron alone – the 355th – claiming the destruction of twenty-nine enemy aircraft. When the fighting stopped on 8 May, the 354th – now based at Ansbach – had claimed a total of 701 enemy aircraft destroyed in 17 months of air combat, more than any other group in the USAAF.

At eight o'clock in the evening of 8 May 1945, two F-6 Mustangs of the 12th Tactical Reconnaissance Squadron were patrolling the Danube when they were attacked by five Focke-Wulf 190s. The Mustangs pulled up in a climbing turn and the leader managed to get on the tail of one of the 190s. After a lengthy burst, the German fighter went down and crashed on the banks of the river while the remainder flew away at top speed.

So to Lieutenant Robert C. Little and the Mustang fell the honour of shooting down the last Luftwaffe aircraft to be destroyed in combat on the Western Front during the Second World War.

In the Pacific the war went on, as the allied ring of steel tightened relentlessly around Japan. On the afternoon of 13 August 1945, fighters of the 507th Fighter Group, 20th Air Force, carried out an offensive sweep over Kyushu. Soon after crossing the Japanese coast the American formation was engaged by a large number of Japanese fighters, and during the ensuing air battle one of the 507th's pilots destroyed five of the enemy. His name was Lt Oscar Perdomo; he was the last air ace of World War II. And the aircraft he flew was a Mustang.

9 Red Falcons:
Soviet Fighters 1941–5

It was 4 July 1941, and everywhere, from the Baltic to the Black Sea, the Germans were on the offensive. The losses suffered by the Russian armies in the two weeks since the Wehrmacht had stormed into the Soviet Union on 22 June had been appalling; hundreds of thousands of prisoners taken, thousands of tanks and guns lost, thousands of aircraft destroyed either in the air or on the ground.

A formation of twin-engined SB-2 bombers cruised at 8,000 feet over the flat marshlands of White Russia, their pilots scanning the terrain ahead for first sight of their objective: an enemy motorized column, reported to be heading in the direction of Krupki. Above the bombers weaved their fighter escort, fifteen sleek MiG-3s of the 401st Fighter Air Regiment.

A cloud of dust on the horizon revealed the column's position and the bombers turned towards it, increasing speed as they began their bombing run. At the same time, the MiG-3s broke formation and went into a shallow dive in pairs, each pilot tensing automatically in the cockpit as the enemy tanks and trucks leaped into his gunsight. German troops spilled over the sides of the vehicles and ran for cover as the leading pair of fighters howled overhead, their guns hammering. As the MiG-3s circled to make a second attack the SB-2s arrived overhead, unloading their bombs and adding to the confusion.

The fighters came in again, speeding through the clouds of dust and smoke that now obscured the column, running through strings of 20mm flak and heavy machine-gun fire. Mobile light flak accompanied every German armoured column and, as the Russians had already discovered to their cost, low- and medium-level attacks could be suicidal affairs.

The leading MiG-3 was hit as it climbed away and began to trail smoke. A moment later, flames burst from its wing and the fighter began to disintegrate, plunging down to explode a couple of miles from the enemy column.

Colonel Stepan Suprun, fifteen confirmed victories, veteran of Spain and Manchuria, Hero of the Soviet Union and commander of the 401st Fighter Air Regiment, had fought his last battle.

In June 1941, when the German armies struck in the east, the great majority of Soviet Air Force fighter units were still equipped with I-16 Ratas and I-15 Chaika biplane fighters, aircraft which had held their own well enough in Spain but which now, four years later, were no match for the latest Messerschmitt 109s. Nevertheless the Russian pilots fought hard, and many were prepared to sacrifice their lives by deliberately ramming their opponents when they found themselves trapped. Early in the morning of 22 June, for example, when the Messerschmitt 110s of Zerstörergeschwader 26 encountered the I-16s of the 124th Air Regiment over Kobrin, one of the Russian pilots, Lieutenant Dmitri V. Kokorev, flew his Rata head-on into a 110. The two aircraft spun down, locked together, and exploded on the ground. No one succeeded in baling out. Lieutenants P. S. Ryabtsev and A. S. Danilov of the 123rd Air Regiment also made ramming attacks that day, as did First Lieutenant Ivanov of the 46th Air Regiment. Ivanov was luckier than most; he survived to be awarded the title of Hero of the Soviet Union.

Of the more modern fighters that were re-equipping the Russian squadrons in 1941, the best was undoubtedly the MiG-3, a redesigned version of the earlier MiG-1. Over 1,200 were built during the first half of 1941, and most were assigned to units defending key sectors of Soviet territory, such as Baku, Leningrad and Moscow. The 34th and 233rd Fighter Regiments were already using MiG-3s in the Moscow sector in April 1941, before the German attack. The 34th Regiment, commanded by Major L. G. Rybkin, was based at Vnukovo, while the 233rd Regiment operated out of Tushino.

Many Russian fighter pilots viewed their conversion to the MiG-3 with mixed feelings, and some with downright distrust. It was a far from easy aircraft to handle, both in the air and on the ground. Taxi-ing could be a nightmare; the cockpit was situated a long way aft and the lengthy cowling, housing the 1,350-hp Mikulin in-line engine, completely obscured the pilot's forward vision. Approach speeds were high, and several pilots, used to the lighter, more responsive I-15s and I-16s, were killed when they accidentally spun their MiG-3s at low altitude. All this earned the MiG-3 the quite unjustified reputation of being a 'flying coffin', and feelings in some cases ran so high that the pilots of one fighter unit, based at Kishinev in Moldavia in May 1941, flatly refused to convert to the new aircraft. The situation was saved by MiG test pilot Pyotr Stefanovsky, who visited the mutinous unit and threw a MiG-3 all over the sky for half an hour in front of the sceptical pilots and managed to convince them that it was not a killer after all.

One unit which had no problem with the MiG-3 was Stepan Suprun's 401st Fighter Regiment. Like its sister unit, the 402nd Regiment, the 401st technically belonged to the Soviet Naval Air Arm, but in fact was directly under the orders of the Supreme Command. The unusual thing about both regiments was that their flying personnel were almost all test pilots, both civilian and military. The idea of forming a nucleus of highly experienced men had been put forward by Suprun to Stalin, who had given the scheme top priority. Suprun was given command of the 401st Regiment and the 402nd went to his colleague, Pyotr Stefanovsky.

Suprun's fighting team, which numbered some of the world's most experienced pilots in its ranks, soon proved its worth. The 401st Fighter Regiment went into action on 1 July 1941 and destroyed four Bf 109s during the first day for the loss of one of its own fighters. During the next two days the regiment shot down eight enemy aircraft for no loss, but the record was marred on the 4th when three MiGs – including Suprun's – failed to return.

Suprun's place was taken by the celebrated test pilot Vladimir V. Kokkinaki, who destroyed a Bf 109 and damaged another on his first combat mission. Kokkinaki, famous for his pre-war intercontinental flights, survived the war and returned to his more normal job of test pilot, flying Russia's first generation of jet fighters.

Kokkinaki's adjutant in the 401st Fighter Regiment, Vladimir Khomyakov, had an extraordinary experience one day late in July, when he led a formation of five MiG-3s to provide air cover for a Russian ground unit engaged in a counter-attack. Over the front line, the MiGs were engaged by five Bf 109Fs; in the ensuing fight, one Messerschmitt was shot down and the other broke away, trailing smoke, with the other three covering it. The Russians headed for home, but Khomyakov, whose MiG was fitted with two extra machine-guns under the wings and therefore carried an extra weight penalty, lagged behind. When he got back to the 401st's base at Borisov, near Minsk, he found that two of his pilots were missing. The furious base commander immediately clapped Khomyakov under arrest on a charge of negligence; he was later released when the two missing pilots turned up, having got lost en route and landed elsewhere to refuel. The incident highlighted one major drawback in Soviet Air Force training: the formation leader was expected to do all the navigating, and was held directly responsible for the safe arrival of his men.

On the southern front, where the German armies were spearing towards the Crimea, one MiG-3 unit which distinguished itself right from the start was the 55th Fighter Regiment, commanded by Lieutenant-Colonel Vladimir P. Ivanov. Many pilots who were to become Russia's leading air aces saw their first combats with the 55th; foremost among them was Aleksandr I. Pokryshkin, who was later to emerge as the Soviet Air Force's top air fighting tactician and second highest scorer with 59 victories, being narrowly beaten to first place by Ivan Kozhedub, who destroyed 62 enemy aircraft between 1943 and 1945. First Lieutenant Aleksandr Pokryshkin was twenty-eight in 1941, and after only three years as a pilot was already a flight commander in the 55th. His first taste of action, on 20 July 1941, was very nearly his last. Together with his wingman, Lieutenant Stepan Komlev, he was flying a reconnaissance mission near Beltsy when the two MiGs were attacked by a squadron of Messerschmitt 109s. Komlev was hit almost immediately and broke away, heading for friendly territory. Two Messerschmitts went after him and Pokryshkin dived on them, sending one into the ground with a well-aimed burst. The next instant, his own aircraft shuddered as cannon shells slammed into it. His engine coughed a couple of times and then stopped. Losing height rapidly, Pokryshkin looked ahead for somewhere to land. Behind him, three 109s were closing in for the kill. As Pokryshkin flattened out a few feet above the ground to make a belly landing, another shell burst somewhere behind him in the fuselage and his controls went sloppy. The MiG slammed down brutally, sliding across the ground in a cloud of dust and stones. The pilot's straps tore into him as the impact hurled him forward and he blacked out as his forehead struck the gunsight.

Pokryshkin recovered consciousness and scrambled groggily from the cockpit. Blood was streaming down his face from cuts on his forehead and one eye was closed. He dived for cover under a wing as a pair of 109s howled overhead; fortunately, they did not open fire and disappeared north-westwards.

There was a village nearby, and an old peasant woman bathed and bandaged the pilot's injuries. Some time later, a Russian infantry column came up and an officer told Pokryshkin that they were surrounded and would have to fight their way out after dark. He advised the pilot to set fire to his fighter, but Pokryshkin refused. Instead, he asked for, and got, the assistance of a team of sappers, who dug trenches under the MiG-3's wings. When the trenches were deep enough, Pokryshkin lowered the

E

fighter's undercarriage, which was undamaged, and the battle-scarred aircraft was hauled out by a truck.

The convoy set out after nightfall, the MiG towed along in the rear and protected by a couple of tanks. Pokryshkin attached himself to a group of shock troops and spent the night making cautious progress across the steppe, with sporadic fighting taking place on the flanks. Reluctantly, before dawn, the MiG had to be abandoned when one of its undercarriage legs collapsed. The Russians successfully broke through the enemy encirclement, but their communications had been thrown into such chaos by the speed of the German advance that it was a week before a dirty, unshaven Pokryshkin managed to rejoin his unit, having been long since given up for lost. Happily, he found that Stepan Komlev had made it back to base safely, having shaken off the pursuing Messerschmitts.

Other MiG-3 units, meanwhile, had been scoring considerable successes. By the beginning of October, Vladimir Kokkinaki's 401st Fighter Regiment had fifty-four victories to its credit, and close rivalry existed between this unit and the 402nd, based at Idritsa. The 402nd went into action on 3 July 1941 and destroyed six enemy aircraft, followed by a similar number the next day. The regiment's primary task was close support and low-level fighter reconnaissance, and its pilots had orders to avoid combat if possible – but the 402nd's adjutant, Major K. A. Gruzdev, devised tactics to bring the enemy to battle. These involved a steep spiral climb to between 15,000 and 18,000 feet, where the MiG-3 enjoyed a performance advantage. The German pilots almost always followed the spiral, doubtless believing that they were chasing a novice instead of an aerobatic champion, which Gruzdev had been before the war. They discovered their mistake too late when Gruzdev stall-turned out of the climb and shot them down. By the end of 1941, this talented pilot had nineteen confirmed victories to his credit.

The most successful MiG-3 unit in the Moscow sector during the first months of the war was Major Rybkin's 34th Fighter Regiment, which included several leading air aces among its pilots. The top-scorer in 1941 was Lieutenant Stepan I. Platov, with twenty victories, followed by Lieutenants N. E. Tarankantchikov with ten and Semyon D. Baykov with nine. Because of its wide combat radius and high speed, at least compared with other Soviet fighters, the MiG-3 was used frequently for fast tactical reconnaissance. Aleksandr Pokryshkin flew regular reconnaissance sorties, particularly during November 1941, when Field Marshal Ewald von Kleist's 1st Panzer Army was pushing through the Donets Basin towards Rostov, the gateway to the vital oilfields of the Caucasus. During the third week of November a dense blanket of fog rolled down across the steppes, with heavy falls of snow, and the Russians lost contact with the Panzers. They had no way of knowing where von Kleist would strike.

On 20 November, Pokryshkin volunteered to fly a lone reconnaissance mission in a bid to locate the German armour. Although the weather conditions made flying suicidal, permission was granted and he took off, flying westwards at low altitude in a blinding snowstorm. With the snow and the fog it was impossible to see a thing, and after flying in circles over enemy-occupied territory for what seemed an eternity Pokryshkin decided to abandon the search and head for home. At that moment, purely by chance, he spotted a series of marks on the snow-covered ground through a gap in the murk and identified them as tank-tracks. Following the lines, he swept over a clump of trees – and then, carefully camouflaged on the fringes of a wood, he saw von Kleist's tanks; hundreds of them. Light flak started to come up and Pokryshkin roared away into the fog, his one concern now to get back safely with the news. When he landed back at his base there were no more than a few pints of fuel left in his tanks. Thanks to the information Pokryshkin brought back, the Russians were able to deploy five field armies in time to make a strong counter-attack, and although the Germans captured Rostov it was retaken by the Soviet 9th and 56th Armies on 28 November. In recognition of the vital part he had played, Pokryshkin was awarded the Order of Lenin, the first of three similar awards bestowed on him during his career as a fighter pilot. During that career, he also became a

127

Fighter!

Hero of the Soviet Union three times. The gold star medal of a Hero of the Soviet Union was – and is – Russia's highest award for gallantry, and only one other Soviet fighter pilot, Ivan Kozhedub, was destined to win this honour three times over.

During the winter of 1941–2, the 55th Fighter Regiment was engaged in bitter air fighting over the River Mius, west of Rostov. During these operations, Pokryshkin took the opportunity to initiate many new pilots into the finer techniques of air combat, taking them along as his own wingmen until they knew the ropes. He strove ceaselessly to perfect his own combat methods, paying attention to the Luftwaffe's tactics. The young pilots who came under his wing were often puzzled at first by his advice: 'Always think and act as though tomorrow were here today,' but after a taste of high-speed combat they learned just how sound this maxim was. At the end of the day, Pokryshkin would assemble the pilots of his flight in his tent – which was littered with the diagrams of air combat manoeuvres he had worked out – and they would talk tactics for hours.

The soundness of Pokryshkin's instruction was demonstrated by one fact alone. Thirty of the pilots who saw their first action with him subsequently became Heroes of the Soviet Union, and six won the coveted gold star twice over. Between them, the thirty destroyed five hundred enemy aircraft before the end of hostilities.

One of Pokryshkin's pilots who was quickly singled out as a natural leader was Aleksandr F. Klubov, who flew his first combat sortie in the summer of 1942. Although aggressive, Klubov remained completely unruffled even during the most hectic air combats. On one occasion, he set off on a lone reconnaissance mission and became overdue. Pokryshkin, who had remained at base, tried to call him up over the R/T and eventually made contact, asking Klubov what was going on. 'I'm in the middle of a scrap,' was the laconic reply.

As dusk was falling, Klubov's fighter appeared over the airfield, behaving very erratically. It was pitching violently, as though on a switchback. Klubov made his approach, gunning the engine from time to time, and brought the fighter down on its belly with a terrific crash. He climbed from the cockpit, unhurt, as the other pilots – including Pokryshkin – came running up. The aircraft was a complete write-off; it was riddled from end to end with cannon shell and MG bullet-holes. Klubov explained that he had been bounced by six Messerschmitts and that he had shot down two of them before a third had shot his elevator controls. Nevertheless, he had managed to make his escape and had kept the aircraft flying by careful use of the throttle, cramming on power to bring the nose up when the aircraft showed signs of going into a dive. A lesser pilot would have baled out.

Aleksandr Klubov destroyed thirty-one enemy aircraft between August 1942 and November 1944, when he was killed in a flying accident. He was posthumously awarded a second gold star.

The first Russian fighter pilot to be awarded two gold stars was a naval officer, Boris F. Safonov, who had scored twenty-two victories by March 1942. He commanded the 72nd Fighter Regiment, which was based near Murmansk in north Russia and which, early in 1942, was equipped with Curtiss P-40s and Hawker Hurricanes, supplied under lease-lend.

The unserviceability rate among the 72nd's P-40s was high, and when the fighters were ordered to provide air cover for the incoming convoy PQ 16 on 30 May 1942, only four aircraft could be made airworthy. The convoy, which was sixty miles offshore, was being savagely attacked by forty German bombers escorted by Messerschmitt 109s of the Luftwaffe's JG 5 Polar Wing, and the four Russian fighters, led by Safonov, raced up to intercept. The other three P-40s were flown by Lieutenants Kukharenko, Pokrovsky and Orlov; the former was compelled to return to base with engine trouble, reducing the fighter force to three machines. In spite of the formidable odds, the Russians did not hesitate to attack; Pokrovsky and Orlov shot down a Junkers apiece and Safonov bagged two. He had just damaged a third when he radioed that his engine had been hit and that he was going to have to ditch. The crew of a Russian destroyer, escorting the convoy, saw him glide down and hit the sea about

129

two miles away. The warship raced to the spot but Safonov had gone, dragged down into the icy depths of the Barents Sea in the metal coffin of his aircraft.

One hundred P-40s were supplied to the USSR, and gave good service on the northern front until replaced by more modern Soviet types late in 1942. Another American type delivered to the Soviet Air Force in 1942 was the Bell P-39 Airacobra, which the Russians used with great success in the ground-attack role. One of the first units to re-equip with the Airacobra was the 16th Guards Fighter Regiment, an elite formation which played no small part in the fierce fighting on the southern front at the end of 1942. The 16th was commanded by Lieutenant-Colonel Nikolai V. Isayev, and his squadron commanders included some of Russia's finest fighter pilots. One of them was Aleksandr Pokryshkin, who transferred from the 55th Fighter Regiment in time to take part in the great air battles over the Kuban Peninsula early in 1943.

The Kuban battle, which lasted for seven weeks into the spring of 1943, marked a decisive turning point in the air war over the Eastern Front. For the first time, Soviet fighter pilots established a definite measure of air superiority, and the tactics evolved by Pokryshkin played a considerable part in this achievement. Pokryshkin's formula for successful air combat was simple: 'Altitude – Speed – Manoeuvre – Fire!' Altitude meant that a fighter pilot always had the initiative, giving him an opportunity to select his target with the added advantage that he was free to manoeuvre into the best position to attack from above; speed meant a gain in precious seconds – a vital factor when the outcome of an air fight could be decided in a second or two. It also meant that a pilot could close rapidly on an adversary, with less fear of being attacked from the rear himself.

Using these tactics, Pokryshkin and a number of other fighter pilots – notably Retchkalov, Klubov, Golubev, Mudrov, Bazanov and Semyenishin – added substantially to their scores over the Kuban. Pokryshkin himself destroyed three enemy aircraft in a single sortie, probably destroying a fourth. His Airacobra, distinctively painted with a large white number 100 on the fuselage, became well known on both sides, and on more than one occasion Luftwaffe formations were known to scatter and become disorganized when the pilots heard the warning shout over the R/T : 'Achtung! Pokryshkin is airborne in this sector!' before a Russian fighter had even been sighted.

The Kuban battle was characterized by clashes between large air formations. The Soviet fighters often operated at full regiment strength, flying in stepped-up battle formation. On escort missions, the usual ratio was ten fighters to four bombers except when the number of bombers exceeded twenty, when they were escorted by a roughly equal number of fighters. Offensive fighter sweeps usually involved one 'Gruppa' (three or four pairs, a total of six to eight fighters) patrolling within a defined sector, with a second Gruppa on readiness. In this way a fighter regiment with four Gruppi could maintain a constant patrol over the combat area. In addition, ranger patrols (*svobodnaya okhota*) were frequently carried out by fighters operating in pairs.

When escorting ground-attack aircraft, the fighter cover was usually split into two parts, the close escort and the assault group. The close escort remained constantly near the ground-attack aircraft and flew between 300 and 1,000 feet higher. These fighters had the task of engaging any enemy fighters that managed to break through the forward assault group to present a direct threat to the ground-attack formation. They normally broke away over the target and circled out of range of the enemy anti-aircraft defences, ready to take up their original position for the flight home. Often, if no enemy fighters showed up, the close escort would themselves dive down to strafe targets on the ground.

The fighters of the assault group flew between 1,500 and 3,000 feet higher than the close escort, and either directly above or half a mile ahead of the attack formation. One pair was usually sent out in advance to scout for enemy fighters, while a second pair cruised at high altitude, up-sun of the attack formation, ready to dive out of the sun on enemy fighters. Over the target, the assault group usually went up to 10,000 feet or so, clear of the light flak, and patrolled the sky over a fixed sector until they were required to cover the withdrawal of the ground-attack aircraft. Changes in the strength of the escort, which were dependent on such factors as distance to the target, the weather and expected enemy opposition as well as the size of the bomber formation, did not influence these tactics. When a reduction in strength had to be made, an equal number of fighters was withdrawn from the close escort and the assault group. If it was necessary to increase the size of the escort, this was done by slotting in additional formations of fighters ahead of, behind or below the ground-attack aircraft.

The battle for the Kuban Peninsula began just as the German 6th Army was being annihilated in the Stalingrad pocket. The fighting in this sector, too, produced its quota of Russian air aces. The first big air battle over Stalingrad took place on 23 August 1942, when two hundred German bombers – escorted by fifty Messerschmitt 109s – attacked the city. They were intercepted by fighters of the 102nd Air Division, whose primary task was the air defence of the city itself. Although this first air battle was inconclusive, by the time the last German resistance in Stalingrad ended on 2 February 1943, 336 enemy aircraft had been destroyed by the division's pilots.

One of the 102nd's leading pilots was Mikhail Baranov of the 183rd Air Regiment, who shot down twenty-six enemy aircraft before his death in action in 1943. On one occasion, leading a flight of four Yak-1 fighters over the city, he ran headlong into a formation of twenty-five Messerschmitt 109s and engaged them without hesitation, shooting down three before running out of ammunition. Then, skilfully manoeuvring his aircraft on to the tail of a fourth 109, he closed in and chopped off the fin of the enemy fighter with his propeller, afterwards making a successful forced landing.

Other pilots who rose to fame over Stalingrad were Sergeant Nagorny, who engaged four enemy fighters single-handed and shot down two of them; Riazanov, Makarov, Piatov, Shestakov, Tchembarov and Alelyukhin. The latter went on to become the

Soviet Union's fifteenth-ranking ace, with a score of forty kills. Another notable pilot, who belonged to the same air regiment as Alelyukhin, was Vladimir Lavrinenkov, who shot down sixteen enemy aircraft in one month over the Volga front and whose total score was thirty-five.

The winter of 1942 showed that Russian fighter pilots could match, and often outfight, their German counterparts. The days when Luftwaffe aces could notch up fantastic scores against inexperienced, poorly trained enemies were gone forever; and now, in the spring of 1943, Russian fighter squadrons were beginning to receive equipment that was more than a match for the Messerschmitt 109, and which was capable of meeting the latest Focke-Wulf 190s on equal terms. Two new fighter types in particular were to bring air superiority firmly within Soviet grasp; the light, highly manoeuvrable Yakovlev Yak-9 and the fast, radial-engined Lavochkin La-5. Both machines were in widespread service by the summer of 1943, in time to take part in the fighting over the Kursk salient – the great armoured battle that marked the real turning point of the war in the east.

The German offensive at Kursk was to be their last, and it was broken in eight days. Overhead, massive formations of aircraft – as many as five hundred at a time – locked in combat. In seventy-six major air battles which took place during the first day, the Russians shot down 106 enemy aircraft and lost 98 of their own. It was during the Kursk battle that Ivan Kozhedub scored his first victories, opening a record that would end with his sixty-second victim in the sky over Berlin nearly two years later.

In the fierce air fighting over Kursk, one exploit stood out above all others. On 6 July, Guards Lieutenant Alexei K. Gorovets, flying a Yak-9, was returning alone from a mission when he sighted a formation of twenty Junkers 87 Stukas heading for the Russian lines. Using cloud cover to good advantage, Gorovets stalked the enemy formation until he was right on top of it, then he dived on the rearmost flight of dive-bombers. Three Stukas fell in flames before the startled Germans knew what was happening, and in the next few minutes the Russian pilot pressed home attack after attack, destroying six more bombers before he was hit by return fire and fatally wounded. He received the post-humous title of Hero of the Soviet Union.

During the summer and autumn offensives of 1943, one Yak-9 fighter regiment achieved considerable success. Although its air-craft bore the same camouflage and red star markings as any other Soviet fighter unit, they carried a distinctive emblem: a white Cross of Lorraine, stamped on their tail fins. The unit was known as the Régiment Normandie, and most of its pilots were Frenchmen. Its official designation was Groupe de Chasse 3, and it had been formed at Rayak, in Syria, on 1 September 1942, with British aid. Two months later, the entire complement of seventy-two officers and men was transferred to Russia, where the unit initially re-formed with Yak-1 fighters.

The Régiment Normandie went into action on the Orel Front on 22 February 1943, under the leadership of Commandant Tulasne, and on 5 April Captain Albert Preziosi destroyed the unit's first enemy aircraft. By the end of the Kursk battle the regiment's score had risen to forty enemy aircraft destroyed, and the French pilots subsequently took part in the bitter air fighting over Smolensk, Yelnya and Vitebsk. During the last months of 1943, they accounted for a further seventy-seven enemy aircraft for the loss of twenty-five of their own number. It was a good beginning; but for the Régiment Normandie, and indeed for all first-line Soviet fighter units, some of the most hectic air fighting was still to come. For although the Russians now held air superi-ority, the Luftwaffe was by no means finished, and during the long retreat of 1944 the Germans were to fight back with a courage born of desperation.

Aleksandr Pokryshkin did not take part in the Kursk battle; his regiment was engaged further south, in the Mariupol sector. Pokryshkin's squadron distinguished itself and was awarded the honorary title of 'Mariupol Squadron'. Afterwards it took part in savage air fighting over the Molotchnaya river, north of the Crimea, as Soviet forces strove to cut off the enemy's forces there. Once this had been done, one of the main tasks of the Russian fighters was to intercept German transport aircraft flying in supplies, which often involved long trips over the Black Sea. On these missions Pokryshkin was usually accompanied by Captain Georgii Retchkalov, and between them they destroyed several Junkers 52 transports. Pokryshkin's squadron also helped to pioneer the use of Soviet radar during this period. The first sets produced by the Russians were primitive enough, but Pokryshkin reported enthusiastically that even limited radar control made the fighter pilot's task easier by half, and during the early months of 1944 a network of mobile radar units was set up along the most important areas of the front.

Early in 1944 Pokryshkin took command of the 16th Guards Fighter Regiment, which by this time had exchanged its Airacobras for La-5s. Soon afterwards, the regiment moved forward to the Rumanian border and operated from the banks of the River Prut – the very airfield on which Pokryshkin had been based when the Luftwaffe smashed the Soviet Air Force on 22 June 1941. The wheel had turned full circle.

In a bid to throw the Russian forces off Rumanian soil, the Germans launched a strong counter-offensive at Yassy, a few miles inside the frontier. To provide air cover the Luftwaffe had assembled some of its finest fighter squadrons, opposed on the Russian side by a number of elite guards fighter regiments. Many of the Russian aces were there, headed by Kozhedub and Pokryshkin; the list of names of the pilots on both sides read like a ' Who's Who ' of Heroes of the Soviet Union and holders of the Knight's Cross.

Inevitably, as they met in combat, the battle of Yassy was marked by air fighting of a savagery unmatched since Kursk. From dawn until dusk, the air thundered with the sound of engines as the Germans hurled wave after wave of bombers against the Soviet ground forces, escorted by Messerschmitts and Focke-Wulfs. The Luftwaffe had adopted the stepped-up attack formation developed by the Russians during the Kuban battle, and initially the Soviet fighter pilots were taken completely by surprise when confronted with their own tactics; on the first day of the offensive, most of the enemy bombers reached their objectives because the Russian pilots made the mistake of tangling with the massive German fighter escort. Pokryshkin's solution to the problem was simple; he increased the number of attacking fighters, leaving enough to tackle the bombers even after the fighter escort had been engaged. The injection of reserves on such a scale was something the Russians could well afford in the summer of 1944; the Germans, on the other hand, could not.

After several days of bitter fighting, the battle of Yassy ended in a clear victory for the Russians. It was the last time that the Luftwaffe would make a serious attempt to gain air superiority over the Eastern Front; after Yassy the German squadrons were shared out piecemeal, and although the pilots still fought gallantly their operations lacked any real cohesion. Moreover, they were up against determined and skilled men such as Aleksandr Klubov, who destroyed nine aircraft in five days. They had been hard-won victories, scored against men who possessed great fighting experience; pilots who were among the last of the Luftwaffe's elite. There were very few of them left now. Many had survived three years of fighting in the east only to give their lives in a hopeless attempt to stem the Allied air onslaught from the west. A few of the men who replaced them were good enough, but most were overwhelmed before they had a chance to prove their worth.

The Russian advance rolled on, gathering momentum in a drive that would take it to the banks of the river Vistula and, further north, into East Prussia. Pokryshkin's 16th Guards Fighter Regiment saw a lot of action during the Polish campaign, and a memorable air battle took place on 13 July. Pokryshkin, Retchkalov and another pilot, Lieutenant A. I. Trud, were each leading a flight of four fighters when they encountered a formation of about forty Stukas and Henschel 129 assault aircraft, escorted by eight Focke-Wulf 190s. While Trud's flight took on the fighters, Pokryshkin and Retchkalov attacked the bombers, which immediately formed a defensive circle. Together with his two wingmen, Lieutenants Golubev and Zherdev, Pokryshkin gained height and then dived into the middle of the circle, turning with the Stukas and opening fire when the opportunity presented itself. He quickly shot down one Ju 87, then found himself in trouble when a Focke-Wulf dropped into the mêlée and got on his tail. Golubev shouted a warning and tried to get into position to open fire, but dared not do so for fear of hitting his leader. The German's cannon punched a hole in Pokryshkin's starboard wing, and the ace's career might have ended right there if Zherdev had not managed to pulverize the Focke-Wulf with a lucky deflection shot. Despite the damage to his aircraft, Pokryshkin went on to destroy two more Stukas; his pilots shot down six more. Shortly afterwards, Pokryshkin was promoted to the rank of colonel and given command of the 9th Guards Fighter Division; he also received the third of his gold stars.

During the summer air battles of 1944 several Russian fighter divisions began to receive a new fighter aircraft, the Yak-3. Faster and aerodynamically cleaner than its predecessor, the Yak-9, the Yak-3 was armed with one 20mm cannon and two 12.7mm machine-guns. One of the first units to receive it was the Régiment Normandie, which used the type to good effect during the fierce air fighting over the River Nieman, in East Prussia, during September and October. The regiment's main opponents were Focke-Wulf 190 fighter-bombers, mostly flown by inexperienced pilots who had hurriedly converted from Junkers 87s and who had no time to become accustomed to the faster and more agile Focke-Wulfs. On one memorable day in October, the Frenchmen – led by Lieutenant-Colonel Pierre Pouyade – destroyed no fewer than twenty-six enemy aircraft for no loss to themselves. The exploit earned them the honorary title of the 'Normandie-Niemen Regiment', and they were cited in a special Red Army Order of the Day, an honour reserved for outstanding achievements in battle.

As the Russian armies hurled themselves across the River Oder in January 1945 and ground their way remorselessly towards Berlin, the Russian fighter squadrons found themselves with a major problem. Heavy falls of snow made temporary landing strips unusable, and conditions became even worse when the first thaw came, for the strips became quagmires in which aircraft got hopelessly bogged down. Once again, it was Pokryshkin who came up with a solution; the fighters would use sections of autobahn. With the central reservation filled in, these could be turned into landing strips some 75 feet wide. Moreover, fighters could be dispersed and camouflaged in the forest on either side of the road. By the first week in February, the entire 9th Guards Fighter Division was operating successfully from autobahn sections. The Russians did not know it at the time, but a few miles away squadrons of the Luftwaffe were doing exactly the same thing.

On 1 May 1945, two Yak-3 fighters flown by Guards Major Nikolai Malinovsky and Guards Captain Vladimir Novoselov swept low over the outskirts of Berlin. At little over 100 feet they roared along the Spree, the broad road along its banks lined with the tanks of the 1st Guards Army. Turning steeply over the shattered cathedral, they levelled out again and flew over the Reichstag. From the cockpit of the leading fighter something fluttered down, unfurling slowly; a red banner. The Guards fighter regiment to which the pilots belonged had carried that banner for three years, through the long and bitter struggle across eastern Europe. On it was embroidered a single word : Victory.

Aleksandr Pokryshkin was not present when Berlin fell. A few days earlier, his 9th Guards Fighter Division had moved south to an airfield near Prague. The Czech capital was the last pocket of German resistance in the east; the garrison held out for a full week after the surrender in Berlin.

On 9 May, the day of the final German capitulation in Prague, Guards Major Victor Golubev – Pokryshkin's wingman during the battles of the previous summer and autumn – shot down a Messerschmitt 109 over the city. It was, as far as may be ascertained, the last aircraft to be destroyed in combat during the European war.

10 Fighters over the Pacific

The Grumman F6F Hellcat fighters of Air Group 15 were refuelling on the carrier USS *Essex* when the alert sounded, sending the deck crews scattering and the pilots racing for their aircraft. It was 24 October 1944, and the *Essex* was one of seventeen American aircraft carriers forming the backbone of the US Pacific's Fast Carrier Task Force, designated TF 38 and commanded by Vice-Admiral M. A. Mitscher. Their job was to cover the American landings on Leyte, in the Philippines.

Seven Hellcats, their tanks just over half full, roared away from the *Essex* and climbed hard towards Luzon island, where twenty Japanese dive-bombers and a strong fighter escort had been reported heading for the American fleet. The enemy attack had to be broken up at all costs, and it was up to the Hellcats of Air Group 15 to do it.

The Hellcats were led by Air Group 15's CO, Lieutenant-Commander David S. McCampbell. Below his fighter's cockpit, twenty-one stencilled Japanese flags proclaimed the number of enemy aircraft he had destroyed so far.

McCampbell saw the enemy formation almost at the same instant as his wingman, Lieutenant Roy Rushing, and both pilots were momentarily taken aback. Spread out across the sky above the dive-bombers were no fewer than forty Zeros. It was clear that the Japanese meant to fight their way through, no matter what the cost, to the big American flat-tops, their decks crammed with aircraft.

Fighter!

While five of the Hellcats dived on the bombers, McCampbell and Rushing sped towards the Zeros, which were several thousand feet higher up. Amazingly, the Japanese fighter pilots made no attempt to break formation and swarm down on the heavily outnumbered Americans. Still on the climb, McCampbell and Rushing each selected a target and opened fire; two Zeros tore apart, their blazing debris spinning down towards the sea.

Turning for another pass, McCampbell could hardly believe his eyes. Leaving the dive-bombers to their fate, the Zero pilots were forming a defensive circle. The two Americans climbed and orbited overhead, knowing full well that their chance would come when the Zeros ran short of fuel and individual pilots broke the circle to head for home. The merry-go-round went on for ten minutes, with McCampbell and Rushing patiently biding their time. Then, suddenly, the enemy circle split up and the Zeros straggled away towards Manila in ones and twos. The two Hellcats went after them, and what followed was one of the strangest combats in the history of air warfare. In a running fight lasting just over an hour, McCampbell shot down no fewer than eight of the enemy fighters and Rushing claimed four. Very few of the Japanese had enough fuel left to engage in combat; one or two did turn to face the Americans, but they were easily overcome. Apart from that, it was a case of sitting behind the stragglers and shooting one after the other down into the sea.

McCampbell's victory underlined the dramatic change in the course of the Pacific air war. Japan's fighter pilots, in the closing month of 1944, were of a far different calibre to those who had swept victoriously to the gates of India and Australia two and a half years earlier. Most of the Japanese aces were gone, swallowed up in the cauldron of the Pacific sky, outnumbered and outflown by men whose growing skill matched only their determination to avenge the savage defeat of Pearl Harbor. A few remained, wily, experienced pilots who were still capable of getting the best out of their ageing equipment and coming out on top, but most went into action with only the bare amount of necessary training and were massacred in their hundreds. It was not

without justification that American fighter pilots, in 1944, termed
the Pacific Theatre the 'Happy Hunting Ground'.

The tide of the Pacific war had already begun to turn in May
1942, when a large Japanese troop convoy, supported by a strong
carrier task force, sailed for Port Moresby in eastern New Guinea.
The plan was to capture Port Moresby and use it as a springboard
for the envelopment of northern and eastern Australia, but it
never materialized. On 4 May, the Japanese were met in the
Coral Sea by an American task force of roughly equal strength.
The opposing fleets never came within sight or gunshot range of
each other; the action was fought entirely by naval aircraft. It
ended with one aircraft carrier sunk and one damaged on the
American side and two damaged on the Japanese side; but
despite the latter's technical victory, the troop convoy turned
back and the seaborne invasion of Port Moresby was abandoned.

Exactly a month later, a massive Japanese naval force bore
down on the fortified atoll of Midway, protecting the approaches
to the Hawaiian Islands. The enemy force was led by four aircraft
carriers, supported by heavy units of the First Fleet. It was met
by a greatly outnumbered United States carrier force composed
of Task Force 17 with the uss *Yorktown* and Task Force 17
with the uss *Hornet* and uss *Enterprise*, supported by Navy,
Marine Corps and Army air units based on Midway.

There were twenty-seven American fighters on the island. At
dawn on 4 June, twenty-five of them – eighteen obsolescent
Brewster Buffaloes and seven Grumman Wildcats – took off to
intercept seventy-two Japanese dive-bombers, escorted by thirty-
six Zero fighters. The Americans met the enemy formation thirty
miles out to sea and gallantly attacked it, but the Zeros swarmed
all over them and they suffered appalling losses. Every one of the
Buffaloes was either destroyed or badly damaged, while three
Wildcats were shot down and two damaged. Soon afterwards,
four Army B-26s and six Navy Grumman Avenger torpedo-
bombers tried to attack the Japanese task force; two B-26s and
one Avenger were shot down, and no hits were registered on the
enemy vessels.

Fighter!

The Japanese, concentrating on the destruction of the air units on Midway, were caught unprepared for the American carrier air attacks, which began at 09.30 with a heroic but unsuccessful effort by the fifteen Douglas Devastators of the USS *Hornet*'s Torpedo Squadron 8. They ran into forty-eight Zeros, freshly launched to provide air cover for the Japanese strike aircraft which had just returned from the Midway attacks, and were massacred. Within minutes, everyone had been shot into the sea, the majority before they had a chance to release their torpedoes.

Then, at 10.15, it was the USS *Yorktown*'s turn. Twelve Devastators under Lieutenant-Commander Lance E. Massey and seventeen Dauntless dive-bombers, led by Lieutenant-Commander Maxwell F. Leslie, located the enemy carriers and launched their attack, escorted by six Wildcats. Massey's pilots began their torpedo runs and the Wildcats strove hard to protect them, but they were hopelessly outnumbered and ten of the Devastators went flaming into the sea. All their torpedoes missed.

At 10.20, the Japanese were ready to launch a second wave of strike aircraft. As the carriers turned into wind the Zeros orbited them, low on fuel, waiting their turn to land as soon as the bombers had taken off. At that moment, the sky was split by the howl of diving aircraft as Leslie's Dauntless plummeted down on the enemy force, followed by fourteen more Dauntless from the USS *Enterprise* under Lieutenant-Commander Clarence W. McClusky.

Leslie, attacking from the east, selected the big Japanese carrier *Kaga* as his main target. In less than a minute, four direct hits from his squadron had reduced her to a flaming wreck. McClusky, coming in from the south-west, directed his pilots to attack the carriers *Akagi* and *Soryu*. The *Akagi* received two direct hits and the *Soryu* three; both ships were torn apart by fire and explosion, sinking later that day.

The sole remaining Japanese carrier, the *Hiryu*, soon showed her ability to strike back hard. Even as American bombs reduced her sister ships to rubble, she launched a strike of eighteen dive-bombers, escorted by six Zeros. Following the *Yorktown*'s returning aircraft they droned towards the American carrier, but radar picked them up when they were still fifty miles away and they were intercepted by Wildcats. Ten dive-bombers were shot down, but the remainder pressed on through the flak and the fighters and three scored direct hits on the carrier. She was patched up and in action again by mid-afternoon.

Her ordeal, however, was only just beginning. Soon afterwards, a second strike of Japanese torpedo-bombers – all the remaining aircraft the *Hiryu* could muster – swept down on her. Five were shot down, but the rest put two torpedoes into her port side. As she was hopelessly damaged and listing badly, her crew abandoned her and she was left to die. She was later boarded again and taken in tow, only to be sunk by the Japanese submarine I-168.

Ironically, it was a reconnaissance aircraft from the *Yorktown*, launched just before the strike that crippled her, that located the *Hiryu* and led twenty-four dive-bombers from the u s s *Enterprise* to her. They scored four hits on her flight deck, setting her ablaze from end to end. With uncontrollable fires raging throughout her hull, she was abandoned and sunk by Japanese destroyers early on 5 June. So perished the last of Admiral Chuichi Nagumo's fast carrier force, which had dealt such a blow to American pride only seven months earlier; and with her perished Japan's hopes of further expansion in the Pacific. In addition to the carriers, the Japanese had lost one heavy cruiser and 258 aircraft, together with a large percentage of their most experienced naval pilots. It was a decisive defeat from which the Japanese were never to recover.

For America, the long fight back across the Pacific began on 7 August 1942, when a division of United States Marines stormed ashore on Guadalcanal in the Solomon Islands. One of the primary objectives was an airfield the Japanese had built; the Marines moved in and took it, and the land battle subsequently centred on this vital jungle airstrip, renamed Henderson Field by the Americans. The Marines hung on desperately in one of the most tenacious and heroic actions of the Pacific war, and by

Fighter !

20 August the strip had been made secure enough for the first American fighters to fly in.

They were the Wildcats of Marine Fighter Squadron VMF-223, led by Major John L. Smith, and they were followed by Major Robert E. Galer's VMF-224 a few days later. The day after their arrival, VMF-223 intercepted six Zeros at 14,000 feet; Smith shot down one of them, drawing first blood for the squadron. The following afternoon the Japanese came again, this time with fifteen bombers escorted by twelve Zeros. All of VMF-223's serviceable Wildcats rose to intercept the enemy, and in the course of a savage air battle over the island they destroyed sixteen Japanese aircraft for the loss of three Wildcats. John Smith and one of his flight commanders, Captain Marion E. Carl, each shot down three.

Day after day, while the ground forces strove desperately to hold the thin perimeter around Henderson Field, the Marine pilots went into action against the enemy squadrons that made determined attempts to wipe out the primitive airstrip, Japanese warships shelled the base every night, and individual enemy aircraft carried out nuisance raids to ensure that the American pilots got little rest. As the weeks went by, malaria, dysentery and fatigue began to have a telling effect, yet the Americans, flying to the limits of their physical endurance, somehow managed to retain air superiority. By the time VMF-223 was relieved in October, the pilots had destroyed 110 enemy aircraft; John Smith's score was nineteen, while his close rival Marion Carl had shot down sixteen. Major Robert E. Galer, of VMF-224, had chalked up thirteen victories; both he and Smith were awarded the Congressional Medal of Honour.

The replacement squadrons on Guadalcanal were VMF-121 and VMF-212. One of the former's pilots was Captain Joe Foss, a farm boy from South Dakota whose marksmanship – thanks to his father's tuition with rifle and shotgun – was superb. Foss had his first joyride while working his way through Sioux Falls College, and from that moment on his one goal was to be a pilot. He spent every dollar on flying lessons, and on graduating from the University of South Dakota he was accepted for pilot training by the US Marine Corps.

Over Guadalcanal, Foss rose to fame with incredible speed. By the middle of October he was averaging one victory a day, and by the end of the month three a day. His two most hectic days were the twenty-third and twenty-fifth, during which he destroyed a total of nine enemy aircraft, all of them Zeros. On the first day, he shot a Zero off the tail of a Wildcat, then knocked out a second as it rolled across his nose. A third Zero pulled up in a loop ahead of him; Foss caught it at the top of the manoeuvre and his bullets found its fuel tank, tearing it apart. Two more fighters came at him head-on, breaking in opposite directions at the last moment. Foss went after the right-hand one and got it with a deflection shot as it turned. His first victim on the twenty-fifth was a Zero which pulled straight up in front of him; his bullets tore it in half and the pilot baled out. He shot down a second fighter minutes later, followed by three more in the afternoon. His final victim had just destroyed a Wildcat and was indulging in a victory roll, an unforgiveable manoeuvre in air combat. Foss caught him right in the middle of it and blew him apart.

By the time VMF-121 left Guadalcanal in January 1943 its pilots had destroyed 123 Japanese aircraft for the loss of 14 Wildcats. Joe Foss's personal score was twenty-six which made him the first American pilot to equal the score of Eddie Rickenbacker, the leading American ace of World War One. Foss's exploit earned him the Congressional Medal of Honor. He never flew in combat again, surviving the war to become Governor of South Dakota.

January 1943 saw the combat debut of a naval fighter which was to have a significant influence on the course of the Pacific air war: the Grumman F6F Hellcat. Destined to destroy more enemy aircraft than any other fighter type in the Pacific, the Hellcat went to sea with Fighter Squadron VF-9 on the USS *Essex* on 16 January, and despite a number of small early snags the type soon found favour with its pilots, proving superior to the

145

Fighter!

Mitsubishi Zero on most counts and showing a remarkable degree of robustness. Often, during the next two and a half years, Hellcats were to stagger back to their carriers with battle damage that would have written finis to most other fighters. Another Hellcat squadron, VF-5, was formed on the USS *Yorktown* (the second carrier to bear that name) in the spring of 1943, and both units went into action at the end of August, when Task Force 15 carried out a series of air strikes against Japanese installations on Marcus Island.

The first of the new generation of US carrier fighters to enter combat in the Pacific, however, was not the Hellcat, but the heavy and powerful Chance Vought F4U Corsair, which entered service with Marine Fighter Squadron VMF-124 (the ' Checkerboards') at Camp Kearney, California, in September 1942. The following February, twelve of VMF-124's Corsairs arrived at Henderson Field, Guadalcanal, and flew their first mission on the thirteenth, escorting a formation of Liberator bombers in a raid on Bougainville. No enemy fighters were sighted on this occasion, but the Zeros were up in strength the following day when the operation was repeated. Over Kahili airfield, south of Bougainville, the American formation – which included USAAF P-38s and P-40s – was attacked by about fifty Japanese fighters, and in an air battle that lasted only a matter of minutes the Zeros shot down two Liberators, two Corsairs, two P-40s and four P-38s for the loss of four of their own number.

It was hardly an auspicious start to the Corsair's combat career, but as the Marine pilots grew more used to their new aircraft the situation improved radically. During the next few weeks, VMF-124 destroyed sixty-eight Japanese aircraft for the loss of eleven Corsairs and only three pilots. One of the squadron's most successful pilots was Lieutenant Ken Walsh, who shot down three Zeros on 1 April and three more on 13 May. A few days later he added a seventh Zero and two Val dive-bombers to his score. Walsh went on to run up a tally of twenty-one enemy aircraft and was awarded the Congressional Medal of Honour for two gallant air actions over Vella Lavella island on 15 and 30 August 1943.

146

It was the Corsair, too, that brought fame and the Medal of Honour to the leading Marine Corps ace, 'Pappy' Boyington, who took his VMF-214 – the 'Black Sheep' – to the Russell Islands in September 1943. The squadron went into action immediately, fighting a big air battle on 16 September when the Corsairs, attacking enemy bombers over Ballale, were themselves attacked by fifty Zeros. In the scrap that followed the pilots of VMF-214 destroyed twelve enemy aircraft, Boyington claiming five. By Christmas, Boyington's score had risen to twenty-four; he got his twenty-fifth in a big dogfight over Rabaul on 27 December, but oil from his victim smothered his windscreen and prevented him from increasing his score, even though he made several furious, half-blind passes at Zeros which flashed past him.

Boyington's last battle took place on the morning of 3 January 1944, when his Corsairs encountered twelve Zeros over Rabaul. Boyington shot down one of them, then dived down through broken cloud with his wingman, Lieutenant Ashmun, to attack another enemy formation. This time, the odds were too great even for a man of Boyington's calibre. In a brief and savage fight he destroyed two more Zeros, but he and Ashmun were both shot down in turn. Boyington managed to bale out and spent the rest of the war as a Japanese prisoner, but no other Marine Corps pilot was to equal his score.

It was during these early months of 1944 that the United States Navy started to bring the war home to the enemy with a vengeance, striking hard at the Japanese bases in the Pacific island chain. At the end of January, Task Force 58, composed of six heavy and six light carriers under Rear-Admiral Mitscher, opened the campaign to recapture the Marshall Islands with a series of heavy air attacks on Maloelap, Kwajalein and Wotje atolls. With these objectives taken, the carrier aircraft hammered the Japanese naval base at Truk, flying 1,250 combat sorties in two days, and late in February they hit Saipan, Tinian, Rota and Guam, destroying sixty-seven enemy aircraft in the air and over a hundred on the ground. The attacks continued throughout the spring, with heavy raids on targets in the Western Carolines and further strikes against Truk, Rabaul and other key objectives.

David McCampbell arrived in the Pacific at this juncture. At the age of thirty-four he was already a good ten years older than most other fighter pilots, and his naval career so far could hardly be described as adventurous. In fact, it had almost never started. Graduating from the Annapolis Naval Academy in the middle of the great depression, he had learned that the lower half of his class – himself included – was not to be commissioned in order to cut expenses. Desperately keen to fly, McCampbell had applied to the Army Air Corps for pilot training, only to be told that his vision was below the required standard. A year later, commissioned into the Navy at last, he went to sea on the heavy cruiser USS *Portland,* and in 1936 he once more applied for pilot training. To his bitter disappointment, the Navy also rejected him on the grounds of defective eyesight.

Determined not to be beaten, the young man from Alabama went to a civilian doctor, who submitted him to searching tests and told him that there was nothing wrong with his eyes at all. Reassured, he went back to the Navy doctors, and six months later he was finally accepted for flight training. Lieutenant McCampbell was awarded his pilot's wings on 23 April 1938. Any aspirations he might have had to become a top combat pilot, however, were quickly dispelled. In the late 1930s American naval air power was far from being the mighty weapon that would be forged after Pearl Harbor; there was only a limited requirement for first-line naval pilots, and this, together with McCampbell's medical record – which dogged him stubbornly for most of his Service career – confined him to the role of Deck Landing Officer.

McCampbell's big chance did not come until the spring of 1944, when he was promoted to command Air Group 15 on board the USS *Essex,* flying Hellcats. His first action came on 19 May, when he led his group on a dawn fighter sweep over Marcus Island. Even now bad luck seemed to follow him, for his Hellcat was hit by a Japanese anti-aircraft shell, setting the fighter's belly tank on fire. He jettisoned it in the nick of time, and despite extensive damage to his aircraft he remained over the target, directing his group's attacks on enemy installations. The flight back to the carrier was a nightmare, and the fact that the Hellcat remained airborne at all was a tribute to the sturdy little fighter's handling qualities. He landed on the *Essex* with his tanks almost dry, but the Hellcat was judged beyond repair and shovelled unceremoniously over the side.

McCampbell scored his first victory on 11 June, while aircraft of Task Force 58 were pounding objectives in the Marianas Islands in preparation for the American landings. Over Pagan Island, flying under a cloud layer, McCampbell sighted a speck far ahead of him. He opened the throttle and gradually overhauled it, identifying it as a Zero. He closed right in and fired a long burst, and the Japanese fighter fell in flames. Its pilot, apparently taken completely by surprise, had made no attempt to take evasive action.

A week later, on 19 June, carrier fighters of Task Force 58 took part in the greatest and most concentrated air battle of all time. In a day-long action that was to go down in history as the 'Great Marianas Turkey Shoot', American fighters and anti-aircraft fire destroyed no fewer than four hundred Japanese aircraft as the enemy made frantic and suicidal attempts to attack the US invasion fleet in the Philippine Sea. That morning, David McCampbell led eight Hellcats from the USS *Essex* to intercept a formation of forty bombers, escorted by twenty Zeros. Leaving five of the Hellcats to tackle the enemy fighters, McCampbell dived on the bombers with his wingman and another pilot, personally shooting down four of them while trying to get at the Japanese leader. He finally worked his way through to the front of the enemy formation and shot down the leader too, despite the fact that his guns kept jamming. The air battle lasted just fifteen minutes, and when it ended the Japanese formation was scattered all over the sky. Altogether, the eight Hellcat pilots had claimed twenty-one victories for the loss of one of their own number.

Fighter!

That afternoon, McCampbell shot down two more Zeros which attempted to attack a pair of air-sea rescue seaplanes in the middle of picking up some Navy pilots who had been forced to ditch. That brought his score for the day to seven, and the overall tally for the pilots of Air Group 15 was sixty-eight.

Five days later, this score was equalled by a single fighter squadron, VF-2 from the USS *Hornet*. At 06.00 that morning, the fifteen Hellcats of VF-2 formed part of a long-range fighter sweep, comprising forty-eight Hellcats in all, launched by Task Group 58.1 against Iwo Jima. South-east of the island, the Americans ran into about a hundred Zeros, and in the fierce air battle that followed the Hellcats of VF-2 destroyed no fewer than thirty-three enemy fighters. Three Zeros fell to the guns of Lieutenant Robert R. Butler, who was leading the squadron, while Lieutenants (jg) H. R. Davis, R. W. Shackford, M. W. Vineyard and E. C. Hargreaves shot down four each. The total for the fighter sweep as a whole was sixty-eight Zeros destroyed for the loss of only four Hellcats, one of them belonging to VF-2.

While the Hellcats were on their way back from Iwo, the Japanese launched a torpedo attack against the carrier task group. Eight Hellcats of VF-2 were flying combat air patrol over the *Hornet*, and they intercepted the low-flying Nakajima B5N2 and B6N1 Tenzan torpedo-bombers while the latter were still several miles short of their objectives. In less than five minutes the American pilots shot down eighteen of the enemy, Ensigns Paul A. Doherty and John W. Dear claiming three and the other pilots two apiece. The Japanese tried again later that day, this time with a strong fighter escort, but they fared no better. VF-2 tackled them again and sent sixteen flaming into the sea, several of the pilots who had been in action over Iwo that morning adding to their scores. That brought VF-2's total number of confirmed victories in the day's fighting to sixty-seven, a record for a Navy fighter squadron in a single day. The squadron lost only one Hellcat.

The battle for the Philippines saw the combat debut of the man who was to follow David McCampbell into second place in the US Navy's list of aces: Cecil E. Harris. In the summer of 1941, Harris left his job as a teacher in Onaka, South Dakota, to become an aviation cadet. Three years later he was in the Pacific with Fighting Squadron VF-18 on the USS *Intrepid*, and on 13 September 1944 he opened a spectacular combat career when he shot down four out of a Japanese formation trying to attack the American ships. On 12 October he got four more while taking part in one of the early strikes on Formosa, and on the twenty-ninth of that month he repeated the exploit yet again. On this occasion, VF-18's Hellcats were escorting the *Intrepid*'s torpedo- and dive-bombers in an attack on Clark Field, in the Philippines. The Japanese contested the raid bitterly, sending up dozens of fighters. Harris caught the first two flights of Zeros on the climb and shot one enemy fighter out of each flight, and in the course of the battle he shot another two Zeros off the tails of Hellcats. His eventual score was twenty-four aircraft.

During that same week, on 25 October, there came a new and terrifying development in the Pacific naval air war. At 10.53, nine Japanese aircraft swept down on US warships in Leyte Gulf; one plunged into the carrier *St Lo*, causing fearful explosions that ripped her apart and sank her twenty-one minutes later; others slammed into the carriers *Kitkun Bay*, *Kalinin Bay* and *White Plains*, causing extensive damage. Led by Lieutenant Seki, the enemy aircraft belonged to the newly formed Special Attack Corps of the Imperial Japanese Navy. The word Kamikaze had entered the vocabulary of warfare.

Two methods of attack had been evolved for the Kamikazes, and both gave the American combat air patrols a lot of headaches. The first method involved a high-altitude approach at about 20,000 feet; although this meant that the Japanese aircraft could be picked up at long range by American radar, it took time for defending fighters to climb to this level, and the long, shallow dive to the target which followed gave the attackers a certain speed advantage. The alternative low-level method meant that the attackers escaped radar detection until they were less than ten miles from the target, but even if they escaped the air patrols

151

Fighter!

they had to run the gauntlet of a formidable curtain of light flak, and since evasive manoeuvres were out of the question because of the need for a straight run to the target, this was a suicidal undertaking. The ideal solution was to combine both high- and low-level attack methods, but the Japanese never had enough aircraft available to make this a serious proposition.

The Kamikaze attacks on us naval forces off the Philippines came as a profound shock to the Americans, and exacted a fearful toll in terms of men and material. Nevertheless, they cost the Japanese nearly three hundred aircraft, and this was a rate of attrition that could not be supported for long. The last attack in the Philippines came on 5 January 1945, when twenty-eight Kamikazes struck at American naval forces in Lingayen Gulf. Seven vessels were damaged, but when the attack was over enemy air resistance in the Philippines was at an end. Not even a single Zero remained.

The first weeks of 1945 saw a considerable expansion of Kamikaze operations, which were to become the main threat to the us task forces in their final drive towards Japan. The threat would have been even greater had not the Americans now been in a position to launch massive air strikes against the bases from which the Kamikazes operated. In three weeks of continual action during January, for example, Task Force 38, with eight heavy and four light carriers, struck Formosa, the Ryukus, Luzon, Okinawa, Hong Kong and the China Coast, destroying over six hundred enemy aircraft. These operations were a preliminary to the Marine Corps assault on Iwo Jima in February, which was covered by the eleven heavy and five light carriers of Task Force 58. During the Iwo Jima operation, aircraft of TF 58 hit airfields in the Tokyo area, the Ryukus and Okinawa, leaving behind 648 enemy aircraft destroyed.

The Japanese, however, still had the ability to hit back hard. On 21 February 1945, thirty-two Kamikazes drawn from Admiral Kimpei Teraoka's Third Air Fleet took off from the shattered airfields near Tokyo, refuelled at Hachijo Jima, and then set course for their objective, the invasion fleet off Iwo.

The Kamikazes attacked at dusk and took the Americans by surprise, sinking the escort carrier *Bismarck Sea*, seriously damaging the *Saratoga* and slightly damaging the *Lunga Point*.

On 11 March, the Kamikazes tried for what might have been a spectacular success when a reconnaissance aircraft confirmed that the carriers of Task Force 58 were refuelling and replenishing in a deep water anchorage at Ulithi Atoll, in the Carolines. Twenty-four twin-engined Ginga ('Frances') bombers, each carrying a 2,000-lb bomb and piloted by a Kamikaze, took off from Kanoya, on Kyushu, and set off on the 1,500-mile one-way trip. Thirteen aircraft, dropped out en route for various reasons, but the eleven others arrived over Ulithi after a flight of almost twelve hours to find the American warships brightly lit. Since they were well outside the combat area, the Americans had taken no blackout precautions.

The Gingas dived on their targets, but only one hit its objective: the carrier USS *Randolph*. Most of the crew were watching a film when the Ginga smashed into the flight deck with a terrific explosion. The damage caused was serious enough, but the carrier was seaworthy again within a few days.

The fast carriers of Task Force 58 were back in action on 18 March, their aircraft carrying out a series of devastating strikes on Kyushu as a preliminary to the invasion of Okinawa. In reply, about fifty Kamikazes – including, for the first time, rocket-propelled Okha piloted bombs – struck at the US fleet and damaged the carriers *Essex*, *Franklin*, *Wasp* and *Enterprise*. Japanese air opposition over Okinawa intensified during April and continued through to June, during which period the US Navy took the heaviest punishment in its history. Although Task Force 58 lost no ships during the Okinawa campaign, one light and eight heavy carriers were hit and damaged by Kamikazes. The Americans had now been joined by a British Task Force, built around four carriers and designated TF 57, and these too felt the weight of the Kamikaze attacks during the Okinawa landings. Although suicide aircraft struck all four British carriers, the latter had more heavily armoured decks than their American counterparts and in most cases the Kamikazes just bounced off into the sea.

It was during the Okinawa campaign that the u s Navy's third-ranking fighter ace, Lieutenant Eugene A. Valencia, scored his greatest successes. Valencia had already flown one combat tour, destroying seven enemy aircraft, and when he returned to the combat area with Fighting Squadron V F-9 in the spring of 1945 he had a thorough grasp of Japanese fighting tactics. He found three other pilots who were willing to practice his own tactics to perfection, and turned them into a formidable fighting team; their names were James E. French, Clinton L. Smith and Harris Mitchell. The team went into action together for the first time in February 1945 over Tokyo, and immediately proved its efficiency by shooting down six Japanese aircraft.

On the morning of 17 April, the four pilots set out to attack Japanese Kamikaze bases on Kyushu. They never arrived. En route, they ran into between twenty and thirty Japanese fighters. The Americans had the height advantage, and Valencia put his combat tactics into practice with dramatic results. The four Hellcats dived on the enemy in pairs, in line astern, making one brief firing pass and then climbing to repeat the process. In minutes, they sent fourteen Japanese aircraft flaming into the sea. Valencia himself claimed six, French knocked down four, Mitchell got three and Smith one. On 4 May, off Okinawa, the team claimed eleven more victories, followed by another ten on the eleventh. When the four pilots finally ended their combat tour, Valencia had a total of twenty-three kills, French eleven, Mitchell ten and Smith six.

After Okinawa, the full weight of the allied carrier task forces was turned against the Japanese home islands, with heavy air strikes on enemy airfields, installations and shipping. At 6.35 a.m. on 15 August, following the dropping of the atomic bombs on Hiroshima and Nagasaki, Admiral Halsey, commanding the u s Third Fleet, ordered the cessation of all offensive air operations.

When the order reached the task forces off Japan, the first

strike of the day was already hitting air bases near Tokyo. The rearmost wave consisted of the Grumman Avengers of No. 820 Squadron, Fleet Air Arm, from the British carrier HMS *Indefatigable*, which were attacked by about fifteen Zeros in the target area. The Japanese fighters were immediately overwhelmed by the Avengers' escort, the Seafires of Nos 887 and 894 Squadrons, who shot down eight of the enemy for the loss of one of their own number. As far as may be ascertained, this was the last time that fighters met in combat during World War Two.

And yet it was left to the Japanese to make the last, defiant gesture. The following day, thirty Kamikazes, mostly Zeros, led by the Chief of Staff of the 5th Air Squadron, dived on the American base of Okinawa and smashed themselves to destruction. A second formation from the same unit flew out over the sea, into the sunrise, until the Japanese coast was far behind them. Then, one by one, they made their last, headlong plunge beneath the waves.

11 Jets over Germany

For Flight Lieutenant Alan Wall, it was just another routine reconnaissance mission. Early that morning, 25 July 1944, he had taken off in his Mosquito of No. 544 Squadron, RAF, from the tranquil airfield of Benson in Oxfordshire to carry out a photographic sortie over Munich. Wall had flown many such missions before, mostly without incident; at 30,000 feet, the fast, twin-engined Mosquito was virtually immune from interception by the Luftwaffe's Messerschmitt 109s and Focke-Wulf 190s.

Today, however, was to be dramatically different. As the Mosquito approached Munich, Wall's navigator gave a sudden shout of alarm as he sighted a twin-engined aircraft closing very rapidly 400 yards astern. Wall at once applied full power, but the enemy aircraft quickly overtook the Mosquito and opened fire. Wall took violent evasive action and shook off the fighter three times, but each time it overhauled the Mosquito at near-phenomenal speed and closed in again, cannon blazing. Several of its shells struck home as Wall hurled the Mosquito into the shelter of a bank of cloud. He managed to retain control and went on to make an emergency landing in northern Italy.

Wall's description of his attacker caused a sensation in allied intelligence circles. It was a highly streamlined monoplane with swept wings and underslung engines, and it was not propeller-driven. Moreover, it appeared to be a good 100 miles an hour faster than the stripped-down reconnaissance Mosquito, which was then one of the fastest aircraft on the allied inventory.

The worst fears of allied Air Intelligence had been confirmed. After several years of vicissitudes, the Messerschmitt Me 262 jet fighter was at last in operational service.

Design work on the Me 262 had begun in September 1939, a month after the successful flight of the world's first jet aircraft, the Heinkel He 178, but because of delays in the development of satisfactory engines, the massive damage caused by allied air attacks and Hitler's later obsession with using the aircraft as a bomber instead of a fighter, six years elapsed between the 262 taking shape on Messerschmitt's drawing board and its entry into Luftwaffe service.

It was not until July 1943 that one of the Me 262 prototypes, powered by two Junkers Jumo OO4A turbojets, was demonstrated before Reichsmarschall Hermann Göring and other senior Luftwaffe officials. Göring reported on the aircraft's performance in glowing terms to Hitler, but nevertheless the Führer refused to increase the fighter's priority rating and forbade any attempt to put the aircraft into mass production, a decision that was to set back the whole German jet fighter programme by six months. Only in November 1943 did Hitler witness the Me 262 in flight, when the Me 262 V-6 (the sixth prototype) was flown to Insterburg in East Prussia to carry out a demonstration. In the course of the display, Hitler turned to Göring and asked whether the 262 could be adapted to carry bombs. Göring, who some time earlier had put the same question to Professor Willi Messerschmitt, replied that it was theoretically possible. At this, Hitler became suddenly enthusiastic about the whole project. 'At last,' he exclaimed, 'this is the Blitz Bomber!'

Soon afterwards the 262 was ordered into full production by the German Air Ministry, and by the end of 1943 the jet fighter programme had been accorded top priority. December 1943 saw the first flight of the Me 262 V-8, the first of the type to carry a full armament of four 30mm Mk 108 cannon. These weapons, which were to become standard on the 262s, were harmonized at 500 yards and used in conjunction with the Revi 16B gunsight. Mounted in the aircraft's nose cone, the two upper guns were provided with a magazine of 100 rounds each and the lower guns 80 rounds each.

Despite numerous snags, production of the 262 began to get into its stride in April 1944, and airframe factories were opened at Leipheim, Leonburg, Obertraubling and Swäbisch-Hall in southern Germany, while assembly plants were set up at Neuberg and Kitzingen. The construction programme was dogged throughout by the continual allied bombing of the German aircraft factories, which disrupted production and made necessary a wide dispersal of facilities. The original target was to build up production to the rate of 1,000 aircraft per month by May 1945, but it was soon apparent that this figure would never be achieved. In fact, the highest monthly total of Messerschmitt 262s produced was 280 in March 1945, a remarkable enough figure in view of the fact that by that time the German aircraft industry was forced to abandon many of its factories in the face of the rapid allied advances. By the end of 1944 730 Me 262s had been completed, and a further 564 were built in the early months of 1945, making a total of 1,294 aircraft.

Notwithstanding Hitler's obsession with turning the aircraft into a fast reprisal bomber, the Me 262 initially went into production as a pure fighter. It was not until 120 262s had been completed that Hitler asked his chief of Luftwaffe fighter production, Field Marshal Erhard Milch, how many of the jets had been adapted to carry bombs. When Milch replied that none of the 262s had been adapted to the bomber role, Hitler became enraged and ordered the conversion of all 262s as bombers, forbidding his advisers even to make reference to the aircraft as a fighter. This decision led to a heated exchange between Hitler and the Luftwaffe's fighter general, Adolf Galland, who saw in the 262 the only possible means of achieving some measure of superiority over the allied fighter formations which roved over Germany in increasing strength. Hitler however remained inflexible, and Galland was dismissed from his post.

Hitler's order resulted in the adaptation of all Me 262A fighters on the assembly lines to carry a pair of 550-lb bombs under the fuselage, two of the nose-mounted 30mm cannon being removed to compensate for the extra weight. The bomber variant that went into production was the Me 262A-2, known as the Stürmvogel (Stormbird). This was originally planned to have more powerful Junkers OO4C jet engines and a nose armament of six Mk 108 cannon, but because of technical troubles the OO4C engines never became operational and all Me 262A-2s were fitted with standard Jumo OO4B turbojets and an armament of four cannon.

It was as a high-speed bomber that the Messerschmitt 262 first entered Luftwaffe service, the first examples being delivered to Kampfgeschwader 51 in July 1944. Other bomber units equipped with the type were KGs 6, 27 and 54. Problems encountered during operational training delayed the aircraft's combat debut, but in the autumn of 1944 the 262s began to appear in growing numbers, carrying out low-level attacks on allied installations and armoured columns on the western front. One of the 262's most important tasks was fast low-level photo-reconnaissance, and for months the jets roved at will over the entire battlefront, photographing installations deep behind the allied lines and gradually enabling the German General Staff to build up a complete intelligence picture of the allied order of battle in northern France, Holland and Belgium. Slipping over the front line at zero feet and hugging the contours of the terrain, the 262s usually achieved complete surprise and completed their missions before the allied defences were able to react. The aircrafts' high speed made it difficult for anti-aircraft guns to track them successfully, and allied piston-engined fighters could only hope to catch them by means of a dive from several thousand feet higher up. In an effort to combat the menace the allies maintained almost continual air patrols, with their latest fighter aircraft – such as the RAF's new Hawker Tempests – operating in pairs over the front line and a second pair held at cockpit readiness on the ground in the hope of catching the 262s as they slipped across. More often than not, however, the expertly camouflaged 262s, which were extremely difficult to spot from a higher altitude, eluded this fighter screen and got clean away.

Jim Rosser, now a Flight Lieutenant and flying Spitfire XIVs with No. 66 Squadron, was on patrol at 15,000 feet over Venlo in Holland one day in September 1944 when he sighted a 262 a few thousand feet lower down.

'I don't think anyone had actually managed to shoot down a 262 at that time, and I thought this was my big chance. I went down after him, flat out, but he saw me coming and opened the taps. Smoke trails streamed from his turbines and off he went; I hadn't a hope in hell of catching him, so I gave up and rejoined the formation.

'The incident had an interesting sequel. Years after the war, when I was stationed in Germany, I met a colonel in the Federal German Luftwaffe. We had a few drinks and got talking, and it turned out that he had flown 262s. We compared dates, places and times, and by one of those extraordinary coincidences it turned out that he had almost certainly been the pilot of "my" 262. He said that if I had kept after him, it was on the cards I would have got him. His fuel was very low, and he couldn't have maintained full throttle for more than half a minute. But there it was; I got shot down near Arnhem a few days later, so I never did get another chance to have a crack at a jet.'

The 262s' reconnaissance activities increased substantially during November 1944, and the initial success of the massive German counter-offensive in the Ardennes during December was due in no small measure to the wealth of photographic intelligence brought back by the jets. The allies had no aircraft which could achieve as much; the Luftwaffe's fighter force was still strong enough to make reconnaissance missions into Germany a costly business. When the Ardennes offensive opened, KG 51's Me 262s stood ready to lend support by mounting an all-out ground-attack effort, but bad weather brought a halt to operational flying on both sides. In the last week of December, however, the weather cleared and the jets were airborne again, photographing allied airfields in Belgium, Holland and northern

France. On New Year's Day, 1945, these objectives were subjected to a massive attack by Luftwaffe fighter-bombers, which destroyed over three hundred aircraft on the ground.

Meanwhile, in August 1944, an experimental Me 262 fighter unit had been formed at Lechfeld, near Augsburg. It was originally commanded by Hauptmann Tierfelder, who was killed when his aircraft crashed in flames during one of the unit's first operational missions. His successor was Major Walter Nowotny, who, at the age of twenty-three, was one of the Luftwaffe's top fighter pilots with a score of 258 kills, 255 of them achieved on the eastern front. By the end of October the Kommando Nowotny, as the unit had come to be known, had reached full operational status and was transferred to the airfields of Achmer and Hesepe near Osnabrück, astride the main American daylight bomber approach route.

Because of a shortage of adequately trained pilots and technical problems, the Kommando Nowotny was usually able to fly only three or four sorties a day against the enemy formations, yet in November 1944 the pilots destroyed twenty-two aircraft. By the end of the month, however, the unit had only three serviceable aircraft out of a total of thirty on strength, a rate of attrition accounted for mainly by accidents rather than enemy action.

On 8 November 1944, Walter Nowotny was the pilot of one of five Me 262s which took off to attack an American bomber formation. Operating from the 262 bases was now a very hazardous operation since the allies had pinpointed their positions, and for several days they had been subjected to heavy attacks by fighter-bombers. Additional 20mm flak batteries were hastily brought up and organized into flak lanes, extending for two miles outwards from the ends of the main runways to provide a curtain of fire during the jet fighters' critical take-off and landing phases. For additional protection, a Gruppe of Focke-Wulf 190s was assigned to the air defence of Achmer and Hesepe.

On this November morning, in the operations room at Achmer, the German controllers followed the course of the air battle that developed at 30,000 feet over the soil of Germany. They heard

Nowotny claim a victory, and also heard one of the other 262 pilots state that he was being shot down by Mustangs. A few minutes later, Nowotny came on the air again to report that his port engine had failed and that he was coming in to make an emergency landing. Some time later, his 262 was sighted on the approach some four miles away from Achmer with wheels and flaps down and at least six Mustangs behind it. The observers on the ground saw Nowotny's undercarriage come up and the 262 go into a steep climbing turn on one engine. He had obviously decided to try and fight it out rather than land, which would have been suicide. A few seconds passed, then the watchers saw the 262 and its pursuers disappear behind a low hill. There was a dull explosion followed by a column of black smoke. The Mustangs climbed away pursued by scattered bursts of flak, leaving the wreckage of Nowotny's 262 scattered over a field near the village of Bremsche.

Soon after Nowotny's death, the jet fighter Kommando returned to Lechfeld for further training. Most of the pilots had only ten hours' experience of the 262, and the air battles of November had shown that not even the jet fighter's superior speed would compensate for the lack of experience when confronted with veteran allied fighter pilots.

During this training period, one of the Kommando's Gruppen was used to form the nucleus of a new jet fighter, Geschwader JG 7 'Hindenburg', under the command of Colonel Johannes Steinhoff. Although JG 7 eventually comprised three Gruppen, only one of these – III/JG 7 – made real and continual contact with the enemy, moving in turn to bases at Brandenburg-Briest, Oranienburg and Parchim under the command of Majors Hohagen and Sinner. In the middle of February 1945 III/JG 7 took delivery of the first consignment of R4M 5-cm air-to-air rockets; the Me 262 could carry twenty-four of these weapons mounted on simple wooden racks beneath the wings, and when the salvo was fired towards an enemy bomber formation it spread out rather like the charge from a shotgun, increasing the chances of hitting one or more targets. Moreover, the rockets could be launched from well outside the range of the American bombers' defensive fire, the limit of which was about 800 yards, whereas the 262's 30mm cannon were only effective at ranges of 250 yards or less. In the midst of the inevitable confusion and dislocation that followed the discharge of a full salvo of R4Ms into the middle of a bomber formation the 262 pilots were usually able to close in and make cannon attacks without too much opposition from the enemy gunners.

During their first series of operations using a combination of R4Ms and 30mm cannon in the last week of February 1945, the pilots of III/JG 7 destroyed no fewer than forty-five four-engined American bombers and fifteen of their escorting fighters for the loss of only four 262s. There were further successes during March, although the 262s' loss rate continued to climb. On one occasion on 24 March, five 262s were shot down by Mustangs and Thunderbolts escorting bombers of the 15th US Air Force to Berlin. Despite what was rapidly becoming a serious rate of attrition, on 4 April JG 7 launched forty-nine Me 262s against a formation of 150 American bombers over Nordhausen, destroying ten and claiming fifteen probably destroyed.

Meanwhile, in January 1945, permission had at last been granted for the formation of a new Me 262 fighter unit at Brandenburg-Briest commanded by Lieutenant-General Adolf Galland. The nucleus of the new unit was formed on 10 February from the personnel of IV/JG 54, most of whom were veterans. By the beginning of March Galland had recruited forty-five pilots, all of them highly experienced. They included Johannes Steinhoff, who turned over the command of JG 7 to a Major Weissenberg and walked out without waiting for authority from his superiors.

Steinhoff was without doubt one of the Luftwaffe's most experienced fighter pilots, with 176 confirmed victories to his credit. Most of his flying had been done with two elite Geschwader, JG 77 and JG 52. He had scored his first kill on 18 December 1939, shooting down a Wellington bomber of the RAF near Heligoland and after that he had commanded the Luftwaffe's first night-fighter squadron for a time before returning to day fighters, As Galland's second-in-command, he fought on until almost the last day of the war, when his Me 262 crashed in flames. He survived, despite appalling burns, and in the 1960s rose to command the Federal German Luftwaffe. Another talented and much-decorated pilot who flew Me 262s alongside Galland and Steinhoff was Colonel Gordon Gollob, who had amassed 160 kills since that day, four and a half years earlier, when he had battled against the Spitfires of No. 72 Squadron over the north-east coast of England during the disastrous raid of 15 August 1940.

In mid-March, Jagdverband 44, as Galland's 262 unit was known, flew to Lechfeld with its full complement of Me 262s and from there to München-Riem, which was to be its main operational base during March and April. The main targets of JV 44 were the bombers of the 15th Air Force, coming up from the south, whereas JG 7, operating in northern and central Germany, had to contend with the 8th Air Force operating from British bases. Serviceability problems resulted in no more than twenty of JV 44's 262s being operational at any one time, and since the unit's primary mission was to attack and destroy the enemy bombers contact with their escorting fighters was to be avoided if at all possible.

Because of the poor manoeuvrability of the 262, which made keeping formation hard work, the basic combat element adopted was the Kette (chain), an element of three aircraft instead of the more usual Schwarm or element of four. Another reason for the adoption of this three-aircraft formation was that the runways used by the jets were just wide enough to accommodate three 262s side by side on a formation take-off, which meant that twenty-four aircraft could be scrambled within five minutes from the time the pilots entered the cockpits.

In attacking bomber formations, both JV 44 and JG 7 used units of Staffel (Squadron) size, consisting of nine aircraft in three elements of three, employing the ' vic ' formation with one element leading and the other two on the flanks, slightly higher up and to the rear. If more than one Staffel was used the other Staffeln

165

flew on both sides to the rear and slightly higher, or to one side in echelon. Because of the jets' high speed there was no need for top cover. Once the bomber formation had been sighted, each Staffel commander selected an individual bomber group, beginning the attack run from a distance of 5,000 yards and 5,000 feet higher up. On the approach, the basic three-aircraft elements of the Staffel went into line astern, diving to a point some 1,500 feet below and 1,500 yards behind the bombers to gain speed before pulling up and flying straight and level for the last thousand yards. On the last stage of the attack the 262s reached a speed of about 530 mph, more than enough to avoid the allied fighter escort.

In addition to the 262's normal Revi gunsight, which was used in conjunction with the 30mm cannon, each aircraft had graduations etched on its windscreen, spaced so as to frame the wingspan of a B-17 at a range of 650 yards, at which point the salvo of twenty-four R4M rockets was launched. Immediately after the rockets were discharged the 262 pilot would open up with his four cannon, closing in to 150 yards before breaking off. Taking full advantage of the 262's high speed, the German pilots would sweep low across the top of the bomber formation in a flat climb, either attacking a second formation or diving away if the allied fighter escort was too close for comfort. Pilots were discouraged from flying underneath the bomber formation after an attack, as there was a danger of debris being sucked into the jet intakes. Since the 262's endurance was strictly limited, the pilots usually headed for home after one firing pass.

Although combat with the allied fighter escort was avoided whenever possible, the 262s were frequently used against allied fighter-bombers. The jets' superior speed made it possible for them to stay at low level and then climb fast to the attack after sighting a fighter-bomber silhouetted against the clouds or sky above, a procedure that was not possible with piston-engined fighters. Many of JV 44's veteran pilots, in fact, believed that the best value could have been obtained from the 262 had it been operated in conjunction with the conventional fighters, which could have attacked the enemy bombers once their fighter escort had been engaged by the jets. At this late stage of the war, however, the Luftwaffe had too few piston-engined fighters for such a plan to be implemented with any chance of success.

The Messerschmitt 262's potential against enemy fighters was demonstrated on 7 April 1945, when the 262s of Major Weissenberg's JG 7 took on the American fighter escort and destroyed twenty-eight Mustangs and Thunderbolts. However, there was no escaping the fact that on that same day the Luftwaffe lost 183 piston-engined Messerschmitt 109s and Focke-Wulf 190s in what was the last series of major air battles over Germany.

Three days later, over a thousand American bombers launched massive attacks on the jet fighter bases of Oranienburg, Brandenburg-Briest, Parchim and Rechlin, shattering the runways and installations with a rain of high explosive. The 262s shot down ten of the bombers, but with their bases devastated they were compelled to withdraw to airfields as far away as Prague, the jet units broken up and scattered piecemeal. In the last days of April the remnants of JV 44 moved still further south to Salzburg, but the jets were grounded through lack of fuel. Most of the 262s were destroyed by their ground crews shortly before they were overrun by American tanks on 3 May.

A few weeks before the end of hostilities the Germans belatedly realized the Me 262's potential as a night fighter, and a single night fighter Staffel, 10/NJG 11, equipped with the jets in March 1945. On the night of 30/31 March, the unit's commander, Lieutenant Welter, destroyed four Mosquitoes on the approaches to Berlin – the biggest individual victory against these fast, twin-engined light bombers. The next morning, Halifaxes of No. 6 Group, operating over Hamburg without fighter cover because they arrived over the target ten minutes late, were bounced by thirty Me 262s of 10/NJG 11 and eight of the bombers were shot down.

Of the total of close on 1,500 Messerschmitt 262s produced before the end of the war, less than a quarter saw combat. Had the figure been higher, the jets would certainly have inflicted

167

severe punishment on the big American daylight bomber formations. As the allies advanced deeper into Germany, they found plenty of evidence of the devastating weapon the Me 262 might have become. Time and again, during the early days of May 1945, they stumbled on rows of jet fighters neatly parked in the pine forests by the side of the bomb-cratered autobahns, together with stockpiles of R4M rockets, all awaiting delivery to the Luftwaffe squadrons that no longer existed.

For the fighter that had ushered in a new and deadly era of air warfare, it was an inglorious ending.